COST AND CHOICE IN HEALTH CARE

The ethical dimension

COST AND CHOICE IN HEALTH CARE

The ethical dimension

edited by Albert Weale

King Edward's Hospital Fund for London

© King Edward's Hospital Fund for London 1988

Typeset by J&L Composition Ltd
Filey, North Yorkshire

Printed and bound in England by
Hartnolls Limited

ISBN 1 870551 85 0

King's Fund Publishing Office
14 Palace Court
London W2 4HT

Cost and Choice in Health Care is a report prepared by a Working Party on the Ethics of Resource Allocation in the Health Care System, convened by the Centre of Medical Law and Ethics under the auspices of King Edward's Hospital Fund for London.

MEMBERS OF THE WORKING PARTY

Susan Baring	Ethics Committee, Camberwell Health Authority
Patrick Campbell	St Pancras Hospital, London
Iain Chalmers	National Perinatal Epidemiology Unit, Radcliffe Infirmary, Oxford
Celia Davies	University of Ulster at Coleraine
Lesley Doyal	Bristol Polytechnic
R G Frey	Bowling Green State University
Raanan Gillon	Imperial College, London
David Greaves	King's College London
Anthony Harrison	Economist, Co-editor of *Health Care UK*
Ian Kennedy	King's College London
David Kenny	North West Thames Regional Health Authority
Robert Maxwell	King Edward's Hospital Fund for London
Rod Sheaff	University of Manchester
Albert Weale	University of East Anglia
D Gwyn Williams	Guy's Hospital, London

Acknowledgements

Many people have helped in writing this report, and we should like to acknowledge their assistance. Martin Hollis, Ken Judge, Onora O'Neill, Sir Patrick Nairne and Janet Radcliffe-Richards read and commented on the manuscript at different stages, as did a number of health planners whom we cannot name in view of their official positions. Alan Williams gave a lucid and informative presentation to the group on the idea of QALYs. The editor would like to give special thanks to Deborah Fitzmaurice for research assistance at a crucial stage, to Anne Martin for constant secretarial services amid the demands of a busy teaching schedule and to Francine Hunt of the Centre for Public Choice Studies who typed and posted successive drafts with unfailing good humour and speed. Judy Futer at the King's Fund combined efficiency, patience and kindness in arranging what must have seemed an endless series of meetings, and the staff of the Fund provided a warmth of hospitality that turned late meetings and all day sessions into a pleasure.

Hamish Hamilton kindly gave permission for us to reproduce the extract from Volume 3 of *The Diaries of a Cabinet Minister* by Richard Crossman on pages 15–16. King Edward's Hospital Fund for London generously provided funds for research to the editor. Marks and Spencer plc gave research support to establish and service the Working Party.

Preface

This report is about ethical thinking in the field of health and health care. But it is no abstract philosophical tract. It is designed to be of practical help to those struggling with the complex questions of allocating resources in health care and to encourage a wider involvement at all levels in health debates. The questions it raises stimulate new thinking about today's institutional structures. As we proceeded with our work, we became aware that it is easier to state problems than to solve them. However, we were also aware of the opposite danger of oversimplification implicit in the view that there was a moral calculus to which decision-makers could turn when they were confronted by an ethical problem in the allocation of resources, and which would yield mechanical solutions to human problems. Moral agreement on the serious, and sometimes tragic, problems involved in allocating health care resources may be less important than moral understanding, and it is our understanding that we have sought to communicate.

Although as a group we have widely different political views, we hold the common belief that there are procedures and processes that are an essential part of a satisfactory resolution of the problems. Therefore, it is not our objective or wish to endorse any particular set of arrangements. Our real concern is to foster debate about the moral issues involved in allocating resources to health and to ensure that this debate informs the practical conclusions reached.

Abbreviations Used in the Text

AIDS   acquired immune deficiency syndrome

BMA   British Medical Association

CABG   coronary artery bypass graft

CEPOD   Confidential Enquiry into Perioperative Deaths

CHC   community health council

CIP   cost improvement programme

DHA   district health authority

DHSS   Department of Health and Social Security

DRGs   diagnostic related groups

GDP   gross domestic product

NHS   National Health Service

OECD   Organisation for Economic Cooperation and Development

PIs   performance indicators

QALYs   quality adjusted life years

RAWP   Resource Allocation Working Party

RHA   regional health authority

RHB   regional hospital board

WHO   World Health Organization

Contents

CHAPTER 1

Three Examples of the Problems of Resource Allocation in Health Care

In recent years there has been a growing recognition of the difficult choices that policy makers, managers and clinicians face in the allocation of scarce health care resources. New technologies, rising expectations and fiscal austerity make the responsible discharge of the care of the sick a burdensome task. To understand just how burdensome the task can be, we feel it best to begin with some examples, so that in the search for principles we do not lose sight of the dilemmas that individuals and institutions are facing every day.

CASE 1: WITHHOLDING TREATMENT

Mr W was a 62-year-old widower who had retired from his work as a motor car fitter because of vague ill health and tiredness two years previously. He presented with end-stage renal failure, meaning that his kidney disease was not remediable. In order to survive long term he would require dialysis or transplantation within a few weeks. In retrospect it was probably this disease which had caused his early retirement. Except for kidney disease he had no other physical problems. However, he lived in very poor social circumstances and had a history of psychiatric disease. For the previous five years he had been under the care of a consultant psychiatrist with a depressive illness with paranoid features. This had required treatment with drugs which he was still supposed to be taking. The illness had begun after the death of his wife from carcinoma of the breast five to six years ago; before then he had no history of psychiatric illness. He had been very irregular in his attendance at the psychiatric clinic, had taken his drugs intermittently and had been openly abusive to the doctors looking after him.

Mr W had two sons: the elder was 34 years old and married with a family of his own; the younger was 16 years old, attending school and living with his father. The two of them lived in a council house in filthy conditions. The house and furniture were neglected and dirty, there were no clean clothes or bedclothes to be seen and there was no food in the house. On admission to hospital his daughter-in-law had taken two weeks to clean his home. He had no friends, very little

1

contact with his family (apart from the son who lived with him) and no social life. During his admission he was somewhat surly, uncommunicative, and virtually without the ability to relate to others – all explicable by his degree of renal failure, the drugs he was taking for his psychiatric condition and, of course, his underlying psychiatric disorder. At no time was he aggressive or abusive. The members of his family visited him occasionally, apparently as a duty, grudgingly fulfilled, rather than because of a loving relationship.

At the time of his admission, the renal unit was in a desperate situation. In the wake of the Panorama programme on the alleged premature harvesting of organs for transplantation, very few transplants had been performed in the previous months, so that the hospital dialysis programme was completely full. Patients are removed from the hospital programme by transplantation, or by transferring to dialysis in the home, performed by the patients themselves, a process which takes several months. Furthermore, there was a severe shortage of nurses to perform haemodialysis because the number of nurses had been reduced for financial reasons. (It is in fact usually shortage of nurses, for one reason or another, and not a shortage of dialysis machines, often quoted in the press, which gives rise to these sorts of difficulties.) It should be noted that the same nurses also have to perform dialysis on patients with acute renal failure, an emergency form of treatment required for patients who have suffered kidney damage following events such as road traffic accidents, major heart surgery or during severe infections. This form of treatment is limited in time and scope, since such patients do not require long-term dialysis or transplantation.

The social and mental condition of Mr W clearly made dialysis in the home impracticable and his only route to survival was a transplant. There were no live donors for him and therefore he would have to have a cadaver transplant for which he would have to wait for very many months, partly because of the shortage of donor kidneys and partly because of his particular blood group. The outcome of a transplant in his case might have been adversely affected by his irregular taking of drugs and aversion to attending an outpatients clinic. So, the only way of keeping Mr W fit while awaiting a transplant would be dialysis in the hospital unit – a facility which was completely blocked at the time.

The alternatives in his case therefore were to withhold treatment, or to overstretch the capacity of the dialysis services which would mean a complete inability to deal with any further patients with either chronic or acute renal failure. Mr W's case was discussed between the medical and nursing staff, his psychiatrist, his GP, both the hospital and local social workers who knew him, and also with his elder son. It was finally decided not to offer him treatment because it was not possible to provide the commitment of resources to his particular case. He was transferred back to the referring hospital where he later died.

Three further points need to be made. First, as the dialysis unit was unable to treat him itself, his case was discussed with the staff at two neighbouring renal units where the same decision was reached for the same reasons. Second, had Mr W presented six months earlier or six months later he would have been treated because at those times transplants were being performed at a higher rate and there was also a slightly higher number of nurses available to work in the dialysis unit, making it less constrained in its ability to offer haemodialysis. Third, had Mr W's case been that, for example, of a 30-year-old married woman with two children and a husband at home there is no question that somehow the unit would have managed. However, it has to be remembered that in this sort of case the options for types of treatment would have been wider and more flexible.

CASE 2: CONSTRAINING CLINICAL PROGRAMMES AND CHOOSING AMONG CLINICAL PRACTICES

In 1984 the adult cardiothoracic surgery programme at Guy's Hospital was saved from a four-month closure by an unexpected benefaction. The prospect of closing a first-class unit caused all the managers involved to consider their personal positions. Because Guy's is in a RAWP-losing district, all concerned had managed cuts and closures before. What made the heart surgery programme different was that there was no question of closing it on grounds of inefficiency or inappropriateness. The specified aim was to stop approximately 100 patients receiving coronary artery bypass graft (CABG) surgery, because insufficient funds were available to support the level of work being undertaken. The amount of money at stake was a potential overspending of £272,000 in the financial year 1984/85. In spite of the fact that there was little doubt that the restriction would result in a significant number of preventable premature deaths, both medical and non-medical managers were committed to ensuring that the closure took place. What was seen to be at stake were the issues of who ran the hospital and how priorities were to be decided.

There was, however, an interesting contrast between this attitude and the fact that most of the managers would have been extremely reluctant to be involved in curtailing the renal dialysis and transplant

3

programme, which was similarly out of financial control. One reason for the difference may have been that deaths from a reduction in the renal programme would occur in identifiable individuals, while the CABG restriction would result in the premature deaths of only a proportion of those not receiving treatment whose identity could not be predicted in advance. Also, the regional health authority had set a target workload for open heart surgery (475 cases per annum for Guy's), thereby assuming responsibility for the effects of the restriction, whereas no such financially-based target existed for renal failure. There was no doubt that the Guy's cardiothoracic surgeons were exceeding the target set and funded by the region. The renal unit was exceeding its funding, but not its target level of activity. It is not entirely clear how these two factors logically change the moral position of managers, but the managers instinctively felt that they did.

Of equal importance are the ethics of the relationship between officers and the health authority which this issue highlighted. The authority had a clear policy that regional specialities should not be subsidised by district specialities. Yet specific issues such as the CABG programme were blurred for at least 18 months. The district did not have financial and activity information systems that were good enough to support a confrontation with clinicians (who made it very clear that they would resist publicly) and senior managers judged there to be higher priorities for action – in particular, securing acceptance of their strategy on hospital site closures. The choice of what information to collect and present will continue to be critical as the district proceeds with the switch of resources from the acute sector into the priority services. Standard information systems currently emphasise patient activity, waiting lists and similar information. This produces a natural tendency to stress deficiencies in the acute sector, whereas deficiencies in priority care services mainly relate to quality of services which NHS managers are poor at monitoring. It is impossible to be neutral in the presentation of information, yet the more managers 'manage' their authorities by the selective presentation of information, the more moral responsibility they assume for their decisions. And these dilemmas will become even more pressing as the country moves from the closure of anachronistic old hospitals to cutting efficient modern acute services in the quest for a better 'balance' within an adequate overall budget.

CASE 3: PLANNING FOR A CONTRACTING SYSTEM

North West Thames Regional Health Authority aims to change the overall pattern of its services during the next few years to meet three important objectives of national policy:

1   To fund national RAWP, which until recently involved redistribution to the midlands and the north by directing virtually all 'growth' money there and holding the losing regions at or near their current levels.

2   To redistribute resources to districts outside London where the population is growing (unlike that of central London which is declining). This entails net reductions in inner London.

3   To strengthen the priority services in inner-city districts and the shire districts.

These changes will require the mobilisation of some £99m in total over the period. The present allocation is £870m, projected to reduce to £844m by 1994 (all at 1988/89 prices). Urgently needed improvements in service throughout the region during this period clearly envisage reallocation between services, and between districts, of some £73m. Thirty-seven per cent of the £99m (£37m) must come from Riverside District Health Authority which is the largest DHA with a budget of £130m. Its role in the strategy is therefore critical if regional and national objectives are to be achieved.

The NW Thames RHA's preferred approach to the consequences of external and internal redistribution has been to effect the required change in local acute services in London at the maximum possible speed. This view has widespread support throughout the region, including among hospital medical staff. In managerial terms, continuing uncertainty over the future is damaging, and the region is determined to remove it. Worse, if planned action does not take place swiftly, a proliferation of short-term expedient actions will still be necessary to meet the year-on-year requirements of resource redistribution. The most significant contributors to the progress of the strategy are the above-target districts. Those most affected are Barnet (£4m), Brent (£12m), Paddington and North Kensington (£11m) and, most importantly, Riverside (£37m).

While there has been little disagreement about the scale of change required in Riverside, concerns have been expressed about the pace of change and how it can be achieved, and the consequential effects if it is not to be achieved. If it is not possible through redistribution to achieve all that is sought, the lowest priority changes will of course not take place. For example, if the amount redistributed is £18m, only £4m (18 per cent) of funds earmarked for improvements in priority and community services would be available for developments in the provision for elderly, mentally handicapped and mentally ill patients. The objective of the current strategic plan of

5

running down at least one long-stay mental handicap institution and one long-stay mental illness institution would be jeopardised, and it is certain that the service provision for the elderly would fall short of that required in some districts based on anticipated demographic changes.

Were the amount to be redistributed to be only about £10m, then not only would objective 3 (above) be unattainable but also an element of objective 2. The region would obviously have to give the most careful consideration to exactly which services would receive development revenue. Criteria would include the impact on life expectancy, quality of life, recurring use of other health and other agency resources, and any alternative opportunity for patient provision.

For Riverside, the district most affected by a declining resident population and where the order of change is greatest, the range of current services is wide. The present pattern of provision is such that there is a degree of duplication in some services. Riverside contains three major district general hospitals, two of which are teaching hospitals (Charing Cross and Westminster). The third (St Stephen's) participates fully in the teaching of undergraduate medical students and undertakes a significant acute workload. Charing Cross Hospital (761 beds), a new building, representing a substantial and recent capital investment, is increasingly becoming the 'natural home' for high technology regional and supra-district specialties. Westminster Hospital was opened in 1939 and has 413 beds in use covering a wide range of district and supra-district specialties, including radio-therapy and oncology, and has new main operating theatres and a new obstetric unit. The associated Westminster Children's Hospital (61 beds) provides a variety of specialised services including bone marrow transplantation. St Stephen's Hospital (368 beds), formerly a workhouse infirmary, has undergone partial redevelopment; the most recent phase was opened in 1971. St Stephen's has an extremely busy accident and emergency department. Other hospitals in the district include St Mary Abbot's Hospital (218 beds), formerly a general hospital, which has been developing as a centre for the continued care of the elderly and for the elderly mentally ill, including 40 psychogeriatric patients from Banstead Hospital. In addition to two main psychiatric hospitals, Banstead and Horton, Riverside DHA is also responsible for Cassell Hospital (53 beds), a specialised psychotherapy unit with a national catchment area. The Gordon Hospital is under conversion for local provision for Banstead and Horton patients. The remaining hospital in the district, the West London Hospital, provides geriatric and obstetric services.

The feasibility of Riverside achieving full target savings through 'across the board' reductions over all units rather than by closing a large acute hospital can be examined by considering that the combined allocation of the three major units (Charing Cross, St Stephen's and Westminster) is about £85 million. Therefore a target saving of, say, £18m would represent a cost reduction of 21 per cent. A recent study considered the costs of Charing Cross Hospital in order to evaluate the possibility of achieving major savings before a major closure within Riverside was contemplated. There is little evidence to suggest that the hospital is wasting resources on any significant scale. Charing Cross has a high cost-per-case but this is more or less as expected for its case mix (DHSS PIs 1985/86). Cost improvement programme (CIP) savings are possible through competitive tendering, 'better buying', clinical efficiency and so on, but these savings are unlikely to be greater relatively than savings arising from the same exercises in other hospitals. CIPs will not yield the 21 per cent required saving, particularly in view of the fact that by March 1988, £8.2m revenue had already been realised, primarily through cost improvements and better bed utilisation.

To keep Westminster, St Stephen's and St Mary Abbot's open in the medium to long-term would not be a practicable proposition and must be ruled out as a viable option. They could be kept open for about two years, but some strategic choices about the location of particular services which have to be made now will give a strong indication of which hospital will have the long-term future. These doubts could occasion political pressure in relation particularly to Westminster and St Stephen's but would be significantly greater for Westminster Hospital. It would be possible to keep both Westminster and St Stephen's going for two years but plan for one or the other in the long-term. The final choice could be kept open, but only with considerable difficulty.

The most favourable revenue option for both NW Thames and the NHS as a whole would be closure of Westminster. It would also be easier to provide a balanced and accessible service as the resident population is centred around St Stephen's and east-west communication in that part of central London is poor. Riverside DHA is now exploring that option. It comprises a package of proposals through which St Mary Abbot's would be closed and the sale of the valuable site would help fund redevelopment on the St Stephen's site. Once that was completed, Westminster and the other hospitals would also close. The scale and pace of change is substantially in excess of anything previously attempted in the NHS.

7

GENERAL REMARKS

We begin with these three examples because it is in concrete cases that ethical dilemmas are sharpened and clarified. They also bring out the complexity of the issues. What can we say about the examples, and do they have anything of general interest to tell us?

The examples given are typical, not in the sense that they confront health service personnel every day, but in the sense that they are true to type, and bring out the difficulties and decisions that the practice of health care presents. These difficulties and decisions can occur at all levels of the health care system. They are often most keenly felt at the level where clinicians and their staff come face to face with people in need. But these individual dilemmas take place in a set of institutions within which resources are allocated and spending is planned. The hospital, the district and the region all make decisions that shape and constrain choices at the level of individual providers and users, just as the collective sum of individual choices shape and constrain decisions at the level of institutions. Moreover, the health care system is contained within a national system of political and economic decision-making that involves choices between health care and other desirable goals.

The first point to make, therefore, is that there are at least three levels of decision-making: the individual (or clinical), the institutional and the national. By the individual level, we refer primarily to the choices that confront clinicians and other health providers when they face patients. The decision to refuse treatment to Mr W was an individual one in this sense, even though it may have involved discussion on the part of a number of different people. By the institutional level we refer to choices that take place within the planning structures of the health services. Both the Guy's and the NW Thames examples are examples of institutional decision-making in our sense. By the national level we refer to those political mechanisms that determine the organisation, structure and finance of health care and that strike the balance between the priority given to health care and other social objectives. An understanding of the ethical issues involved must recognise these distinct levels of choice, and pay attention to the detailed concerns that typically arise at each level. This is not to say that different moral codes apply to the clinician, the planner and the politician. Indeed the theme we shall pursue is that there are common standards and common procedures that everyone has to accept, wherever they are in the process. But different concerns will be differently experienced and we shall need to acknowledge that fact in our discussion.

8

The second point is that at all levels of decision-making – individual, institutional and national – the problems of the allocation of resources do not arise in a haphazard or incidental fashion. The problems are built into the fabric of the processes in a modern health care system. That system provides its practitioners and planners with enormous power to do good, and consequently with enormous moral responsibility in the exercise of that power. The medical techniques that we have referred to in the cases, renal dialysis and CABG, are just two of the developments in medicine that can have dramatic consequences for those able to benefit and for those denied the benefit. However, the increase in power is not simply a product of medical technique. It is also a product of the modern, bureaucratic state, capable of raising huge sums in taxation or insurance, and with the ability to direct these sums to chosen ends. The power of political organisation requires as much responsibility as the power of medical technique, and both are morally constrained by the limits of human resources. Moreover, decisions at a higher level can pre-empt decisions at a lower one. No money for AIDS restricts the possibilities of treatment, or a shortfall in trained nurses makes it impossible to provide certain types of therapy. The higher levels of decision-making set the limits within which choices are made within lower limits. To understand how we might avoid the unprincipled use of these powers, we turn in the next chapter to a discussion of the sources of constraint and judgment in modern health care.

CHAPTER 2

Why Ethics?

Why are there dilemmas of choice in modern health care systems? A significant cause lies in the ever-expanding range of things that can be done, which pose problems of two kinds. The first problem is whether some therapies or techniques are on balance beneficial. The second problem is one of making choices within the range of activities that are of positive benefit. There are too few nursing staff to manage dialysis or there is a shift of money from one hospital district to another. In general there are more worthwhile activities to be undertaken than there are human, material and organisational resources to support them. It follows from this fact that there are some worthwhile activities that simply cannot be accomplished. Resources put to one use will be taken away from another and the clash of priorities may be so strong that it may be impossible even to undertake some worthwhile activities. Ethical considerations emerge when it is a question of determining priorities.

It is sometimes said that these problems would disappear if more money were spent on the National Health Service, and public opinion polls in the United Kingdom have consistently shown support for greater expenditure (see, for example, *The Health Service Journal*, 1987). Although there are good reasons for thinking that social well-being would be improved if spending were increased on the National Health Service, there are equally good reasons for thinking that this would not solve all the ethical dilemmas that arise in the allocation of health care resources. One reason is that medical technology creates a demand for increased resources as the price for delivering improvements in health. Renal dialysis, coronary by-pass surgery and scanners are examples of expensive technologies that are now part of the routine workings of a developed health care system. As the NHS has matured, so its cost has grown. The expectation of some of the original founders of the service was that its costs would diminish as the backlog of disease was cleared up. The contrary has happened. Health care spending has grown absolutely, and as a proportion of national income: in 1950 NHS spending took 3.7 per cent of national income; in 1985 it took 5.7 per cent (Schieber and Poullier, 1987, Exhibit 3). The United Kingdom is not unique in this respect. Indeed, most other developed countries spend a higher proportion of their national income on health care than we do. Yet in those countries ethical dilemmas concerning the distribution of resources are still present.

This is not to argue that more money spent on medical services always means better health. More money spent on medical procedures may have little effect or may even be deleterious in its consequences. We do not assume in any sense that a concern with the ethical issues arising in health care simply focuses our attention on the total quantity of resources going to the medical care sector. Issues of effectiveness and the responsibility of professionals to use existing resources wisely are equally important. Also important, if it is true that almost limitless money could be spent on improvements in medicine, is the responsibility of patients and citizens to face squarely the issues of resource allocation. Responsibility extends not only to all those who exercise choice on behalf of other people in how resources are allocated but also to the potential users of resources whose choices about the conduct of their lives have implications for the likely demand they will make on the resource pool. The cigarette smoker or the car-driver who drives under the influence of alcohol, for example, jeopardise their own and possibly other peoples' health in ways which may call upon public resources and direct them away from other potential beneficiaries. At a quite different level, the individual elector influences the allocation of resources by voting for one or other political party which may exercise different choices in resource allocation.

A further reason why principles should be explicitly discussed stems from the public nature of medical care provision in the United Kingdom. The National Health Service is a public agency largely financed from general taxation. This creates its own institutional context for decision-making, in which power and responsibilities are exercised. The NHS is to some extent a paternalist system in the sense that choices are made on behalf of people and in which, therefore, the basis of those choices needs to be publicly accountable and justified. The average consultant, for example, controls by his or her decisions a budget equal to £0.5m in a year. The spenders of such sums need to be able to account publicly for what they do, not only in the narrow auditing sense that the money is devoted to proper and legitimate purposes, but also in the broader sense that the activities are seen to be ones worth pursuing in relation to other things that might be done.

A similar point can be made in respect of geographical allocations. At least one of the difficult choices in our examples arose because there is a national policy of redistributing resources between regions and districts. A national health service must be seen to be genuinely national, and this principle has come to be interpreted to mean that the facilities it provides should be available to all citizens on similar terms. Yet in a situation in which health care resources are not growing fast enough to enable the poorer regions and districts to catch up with the richer ones, a commitment to equal access to services of the same quality necessarily means that the NHS must undergo a period of painful redistribution. This takes place among regions, among districts within regions and among services within districts. The ethical dilemma here is that shortage of resources in one part of the system is created by a deliberate decision that is based on principles receiving widespread support. The dilemma is exacerbated by it often being politically and administratively easier to continue to deprive patients who have never had access to a particular level of service than to reduce standards that have come to be accepted, although it may not be ethically defensible to do so.

A final reason for being concerned about ethical principles in the allocation of resources is that good intentions are not enough for public decisions. Many dilemmas are created because intended policies can have unintended results, and these unintended results can often reveal conflicting considerations. Considerations of economy may lead to cancer screening programmes that create anxiety because they lack counselling or support services, and yet it may be difficult to fund the highest quality of service in the light of other calls on expenditure. Should we delay the introduction of a service because it cannot be funded to the highest standards? Similarly, policies to avoid queue-jumping in NHS hospitals may create an incentive to establish separate provision for private patients. Should we prefer integration with some inequality in provision, or separation with the possible long-term effect of creating a two-tier service? Such choices cannot be avoided, and they inevitably pose ethical problems.

There is a useful analogy to be drawn between resource allocation and certain other activities in health care which have previously been identified as areas of major ethical concern, notably research and the introduction of new therapies. In these areas, great emphasis has rightly been given to possible harmful effects and to the rights of the individual who may be subjected to interventions with uncertain and possibly even lethal outcome. The need for new institutional mechanisms, such as ethics committees and drug regulatory authorities, has been firmly established and guidelines on codes of practice have become familiar necessities. Viewed from this perspective, the delay in recognising the need for explicit ethical appraisal in the field of resource allocation is surprising, since in many respects it can be seen as analogous to therapeutic experimentation on a large scale, with unquestionably harmful consequences in terms of preventable suffering, disability and death.

Public awareness of the value-judgments implicit in resource allocation has been greatly increased by the visible strains upon the NHS and the publicity given to 'cuts'. What has not emerged in the debate, however, is any sense of the principles in terms of which a public discussion can take place about the problems arising from the inevitability of priorities. Sober realism about the need to choose between priorities can degenerate into a cynical interest in funding short-term expedient solutions unless an attempt is made to identify and analyse relevant ethical issues.

IS HEALTH CARE SPECIAL?

A sceptic might argue that there is nothing special in ethical terms about health policy. Dilemmas in the allocation of resources arise in respect of education, transport or environmental policy. Social inequalities exist in education, road improvements can save lives and environmental policy requires the virtues of prudence and a concern for justice in our behaviour towards future generations. Why should we distinguish one area of public policy from these others?

The short answer is that we accept that ethical dilemmas are raised by other areas but it is in the field of health policy that we have chosen to focus our own response. However, there is also a more general answer that can be given. Within our civic and political culture people attach considerable importance to questions of health. This is true not only of the obvious large questions of life and death but also of the more mundane ills to which flesh is heir, including impairment, lack of mobility and chronic pain. One reason for this is that good health is regarded as a precondition for the enjoyment of other goods. Because these issues figure so significantly on the agenda of our civic culture, the ethical dilemmas that they evoke are implicit in public discussion and debate.

This special significance attached to health care is also often given as the reason why those professions involved in the delivery of health services work under professional codes of conduct that contain specific ethical imperatives. The Hippocratic Oath requires clinicians to agree: 'I will prescribe treatment to the best of my ability and judgment for the good of the sick'. The difficulty is that this high ethical imperative may be interpreted as requiring conduct that is at variance with the norms that a well-administered health service needs to promote. If prescribing treatment to the best of one's ability means prescribing without reference to the budgetary consequences, doing the best for the person in front of one without regard for the consequences for others, then this ethic may well conflict with a fair or efficient allocation of resources. In this way ethical problems about resource allocation are implicit in the practice of medicine, although largely unrecognised and unexplored.

Ultimately, of course, there is no simple way of insulating public policies that relate to health from other matters. Road safety is relevant to transport policy, public health is a product of environmental and housing policy and positive and informed awareness of the health effects of different lifestyles arises from the decisions made in educational policy. Moreover, the concepts of health and health care are ambiguous or a matter of controversy. To some the idea of health care refers only to medical care in response to sickness, disease or ill health; to others it has to do with the totality of circumstances contributing to a person's sense of well-being; and to yet others, health care refers to a set of practices midway between these extremes. In this report we have focused upon issues that are chiefly related to the allocation of medical resources. In making this decision we do not mean to imply any preference for a particular definition of health or any prejudice in favour of particular ways in which health is to be promoted. However, when considering the issues that surrounded the allocation of medical resources, we found that the problems were serious enough to merit attention on their own. No matter how narrow this focus might seem, judged from a more comprehensive perspective, we have found the problems needing attention and discussion.

WHAT IS ETHICAL REASONING?

To talk about ethical reasoning and public policy is to risk sounding priggish, naive or both. Can these charges be avoided? To avoid naivety we should not divorce our ethical appraisals from the circumstances in which principles are to be applied. For example, if an ethical principle requires agents to be motivated by greater altruism than is commonly found in our society, it is by that token likely to be an unworkable ethical principle – 'idealist' in the perjorative sense of that term. So ethical reasoning needs to take into account the circumstances in which principles will be applied, including the level of technology, the need to maintain organisational incentives and the weight of institutional inertia. However, unless we are like Dr Pangloss and believe that 'all is for the best in the best of all possible worlds', we should recognise that ethical reasoning will lead to a desire for change. Thinking about the ethics of allocating health care resources should leave us with a sense of unease about our present practices.

In many ways the correct antithesis to principle is not practicality but haphazardness. Consider the following extract from the third volume of the Crossman Diaries (Crossman, 1977, pages 593–94), where the Cabinet is considering public expenditure cuts affecting the NHS:

'. . . at 5.30 we started Cabinet again, once more in Harold's room in the Commons. All this morning we had heard announcements about offers from Treasury Ministers and the nationalized industries – how much Roy Mason would offer, the reduction in gas and electricity investment, how much would be cut off the railways. This afternoon we turned back to the public sector and I was the part of the public sector where we had halted on the previous occasion. Instead of doing what he usually did, this time Roy turned to me and I began to explain the situation as I saw it. Within a matter of minutes there was a furious confrontation between us. I explained in answer to a challenge that in order to get the £9 million from hospital building cuts, I would have to make a Statement next week. I could confirm this because only £12 million of the building programme was under my control and the rest was under the control of the RHBs, with a firm arrangement that in the course of this programme they could go straight ahead within the cost limits allowed. I would now have to instruct them to hold back artificially, so the story must come out.

'I said Cabinet must be quite clear that there would either have to be an announcement about this, or I could only cut it back to £5 million and, before we knew it, we were in the middle of a terrible row. I had already said I would no longer ask for the £17 million and that I would try to contain that requirement by cutting my revenue expenditure, but this was regarded by Roy not as a give-away but as proof that I had that amount of fat to take off. We got very heated and finally I simply said, "If the Treasury insists, someone else can carry out the announcement of the suspension of the hospital building programme. It's absolutely crazy. I can only do it if it's part of a general announcement of a general cut and therefore it is all a question of publication and the package we present." Unfortunately, in the course of all this argument I also said that Roy's officials had bullied my officials into consent, but as a matter of fact this was completely untrue. We had known Roy was going to ask for £23 million and we had gone to see him about it and showed him the choice between a six-month cut or a three-month cut and said that in either case we would have to have publicity.'

The most distinctive sense to emerge from this passage is the lack of there being any clear principle of allocation that would determine what the right size of the hospital building programme would be. Given the secrecy that surrounds Cabinet decision-making, it is difficult to know how typical this example is, and of course diaries of former politicians can sometimes be unreliable. Moreover, it may be argued that the passage illustrates the difficulties of achieving cuts in already agreed spending plans rather than giving a fair representation of the usual style of political decision-making. Yet, from what we know about Cabinet procedures in general (Hennessy, 1986), it would be difficult to conclude that expediency, partisan calculation and short-term pressures did not sometimes make decision-making in Cabinet haphazard and to that extent unprincipled.

When we discussed the problems raised by specific examples of ethical dilemmas, there was a general feeling in the group that difficulties arose because there was a conflict of priorities among all those involved. No one, it was felt, was in a position to impose a common set of priorities on different budget holders and, by extension, on all those who were involved either professionally or as relatives. The search for principles is in part the search for a basis of common priorities. Yet this search must inevitably be tempered by the thought that those occupying different roles within the health care system will inevitably have conflicting objectives and interests. Common priorities in this context may amount to no more than the recognition on the part of those involved that there are principles of allocation that have ethical support and justification.

COMMON PRIORITIES AND DIFFERENT ROLES

The problem of defining common priorities for those who occupy different roles is one that needs reflecting upon. Clearly there are many different perspectives built into the delivery of health services. The clinician may see his or her ethical responsibility as lying primarily or solely towards providing the best possible treatment for the patient; it is up to the administrator or politician to secure the resources for that purpose. The administrator, by contrast, may see his or her responsibilities as lying primarily within the sphere of political and financial accountability, with an attendant need to control the activities of clinicians if budgets are not to be overspent, policy objectives are to be achieved and strategies of service orientation and delivery are to be upheld. It was this conflict of perspective, for example, that underlay the second of our opening examples in Chapter 1.

Such conflicts may not be preventable, but there has been growing awareness of the need for some means of arbitration between what may often appear to be totally opposed value systems, and for some method of identifying shared goals and responsibilities which can be ethically defended as being in the best interests of the sub-groups and individuals who comprise the population served. The common goal of promoting health demands a communicable language of ethical appraisal which is comprehensible by people with allocative responsibilities, whether they serve clinical, administrative, or political roles or undertake practical responsibilities which incorporate elements of more than one of them.

In the same way that moral responsibility extends over all people who exercise control in resource allocation, ethical implications are to be found in all types of decisions about resource allocation. No decisions can be exempted. The decisions of a laundry-manager to purchase new blankets, of a clinician to initiate a new surgical treatment, of a Minister of State to introduce a new management structure for the health service – all express choices about relative priorities and all, to a greater or lesser extent, entail evaluations which come within the compass of ethical appraisal. None of these choices can be dismissed as entirely beyond ethical concern.

One way to approach the problems raised by the difference of perspective that the variety of roles in the health service creates is to understand the sources of the disagreements involved. In this context, it is useful to distinguish between customary and critical morality. The principles of customary morality derive from the ethos that is implicit in any social institution where tasks are assigned to different roles. Simply by virtue of occupying a role in an organisation people acquire duties and powers of decision of various kinds. Sometimes these duties and powers are clearly elaborated (in the various professional codes of conduct, for example); at other times the roles may be more open-textured and less capable of explicit formulation (for those who are relatives of the sick, for example). Reflection upon their place in an organisation or institution will provide individuals, groups and committees with a guide to action.

There is, however, another source of morality to be found in critical reflection upon organisations, institutions and the roles they create. Such critical reflection appeals to principles that institutions ought to embody. These principles may be general in character and

17

for that reason it may often be difficult to see how they apply to particular cases. Nonetheless, such general principles are important in helping us appraise the context within which specific role obligations arise. Moral arguments in particular cases are likely to involve appeal to these general considerations, so that it will be worthwhile identifying the principles to which appeal is frequently made. We turn to this task in the next chapter.

CHAPTER 3

Principles

After some early philosophical sparring the group agreed to acknowledge that they were unlikely to resolve any deep disagreements of moral theory. Instead they recognised the plausibility of an intermediate stance for applied ethics proposed by some bioethicists (see, for example, Childress and Beauchamp, 1983). According to this stance, a wide variety of moral theories – utilitarian and deontologist, religious and secular, left wing and right wing – could agree on the *prima facie* importance of four, potentially conflicting, principles: respect for autonomy, non-maleficence, beneficence and justice.

AUTONOMY

The capacity for autonomy – literally self-rule – is one of the defining characteristics of persons. Animals have sentience and are capable of feeling pain, and may thus be appropriate objects of concern and of beneficent actions. But only persons possess autonomy and are thus the appropriate recipients of the particular sort of respect that autonomous beings require. Autonomy may be defined as the capacity for deliberating upon reasons of a general kind and altering one's decision and plans accordingly and acting on the basis of one's decision. Deliberation includes the capacity to think about feasible means to fulfilling whatever desires one happens to have and the capacity to modify one's immediately felt desires in the light of one's longer term interests and what one can reasonably hope to satisfy. An autonomous being is not enslaved by passions.

A useful distinction can be made between autonomy of thought, autonomy of intention or will, and autonomy of action. Autonomy as a capacity has to be distinguished from the principle of respect for autonomy. This requires respect for the autonomy of *all* autonomous beings and thus does not require simple acceptance of and respect for any autonomous decision, but only such acceptance as is compatible with equal respect for the autonomy of all affected.

The requirement of respect for others as autonomous beings is evidenced by our recognising that good government reserves to individuals the opportunity to exercise their deliberative capacities and to act upon their own decisions. Although autonomy is a defining

19

characteristic of persons, it is not an all-or-nothing property. People may be more or less autonomous. If, for example, they have had little opportunity to exercise their decision-making capacity, or have been drilled into habits of unreflective obedience, they will be less than 'fully autonomous'. The requirement of respect for autonomy presupposes only an adequate capacity of autonomy in those to be respected, not the probably mythical capacity of 'full autonomy'.

Autonomy enters into specific issues of health care in several ways. Firstly, we may be concerned that the level of health care and its manner of funding should respect autonomy. Advocates of private insurance provision, rather than national provision, often argue that the former shows greater respect for individual choice; those who favour a national system claim that adequate and secure provision for health care is the only way in which autonomy can be secured. Secondly, ill health is itself a serious impediment to the exercise of autonomy, whether in the area of thought, of intention and will, or of action. Thirdly, in order to restore themselves to full autonomy, ill people are often required to enter relationships or institutional contexts – as, for example, the hospital patient or recipient of similar institutional care – that remove their scope to exercise autonomy and may even finally cause their capacity to wither away. This is a particularly important problem with our care and treatment of the elderly. The obligation to respect autonomy of thought and will is not absolved when people's autonomy of *action* is impaired or even removed by disease.

A development of the notion of respect for autonomy occurs in the idea of democratic consent. Just as autonomy recognises the scope for self-determination at the levels of individuals, so the principles of democracy incorporate the idea of self-determination at the collective level of society. The existing mechanism of representative government is an imperfect method of eliciting consent from citizens. Nonetheless it is an important principle that whatever policies are agreed they should be supported by a broad consensus of those engaged in the finance, provision and delivery of health care.

NON-MALEFICENCE

Non-maleficence may appear to be such an obvious virtue in any social institution that it needs hardly any discussion. After all, the principle that social institutions in general, and health care systems in particular, should not impose harm or evil upon those affected by their actions appears to be uncontentious. However, the implementation of the principle raises important ethical considerations.

What steps are we obliged to take, individually or collectively, to find out whether or not we are imposing harm? New drugs have to undergo stringent controlled trials before they are available for use by patients. Should the same stringency of test be applied to surgical procedures, or is it sufficient that there is a professional hunch that the surgical procedures perform their intended function? Furthermore, there is always a risk of harm from pursuing what is generally a beneficial procedure; to what extent is one in breach of the non-maleficence principle in pursuing that procedure? Any operation inflicts certain harm (damage to tissue, for example) and risks other harms (death under anaesthetic, for example). And the pursuit of benefit for many may risk harm for others – as may be the case, for example, with some mass vaccination programmes. Finally, insofar as the choice of priorities involves the possibility that certain treatments and procedures may be regarded as too expensive for general use, we must accept that the principle of non-maleficence will be breached. If it were accepted, for example, that AIDS cases were not to be treated on grounds of expense, then it would be appropriate to say that such patients had been harmed by a decision on the allocation of resources. We find, then, that even if the principle of non-maleficence is uncontentious in the abstract, its application poses some interesting and intriguing problems.

BENEFICENCE

Beneficence is a more positive notion than non-maleficence. It requires that people, and social institutions on their behalf, pursue beneficial goals and enjoins the increase of good over harm. Some moral theories, notably utilitarianism, elevate beneficence to the supreme moral obligation. Their health care applications usually require the maximisation of some quantity – the number of patients treated or years of life prolonged for example. But beneficence need not be seen as a maximising requirement. At some level or other an obligation to benefit others seems to be an uncontentious virtue except when it comes into conflict with other principles. Because of such conflict, the duties it implies require careful specification, otherwise it may threaten to absorb the energies and talents of medical providers, and the resources of the community to an extreme and unjust extent. There will always be reason for saying that the marginal benefit to an extra unit of work will outweigh the marginal cost, unless one is careful to specify what in justice is owed to health care providers and the providers of the required resources.

JUSTICE

People appeal to principles of justice when they wish to claim what is their due, that is to say what others ought to yield by way of duty. Although the quality of mercy is not strained, the virtue of justice must be, since it adjudicates between rival and incompatible claims. The formal principles of justice state that each person must be given his or her due and equals must be treated equally. Although formal in nature these principles have had force historically in arguments about the distribution of resources. Where racial discrimination occurs, for example, it will be in breach of these formal require- ments, and appeal to these principles provides a powerful argument for ending the injustice. Theories of justice fill out this formal account by explaining the basis on which the due of each person may be calculated and by identifying those characteristics of persons that form the basis for equal treatment. Each theory offers an account of how a person's due is to be assessed and what makes for just treatment.

However, instead of working from abstract theory to concrete application, it is possible to approach the problem of justice in health care by another route, and ask what notions of justice are embodied in the institutional morality of modern health care systems, only taking up later the question as to whether these institutionally embodied principles correspond to a particular theory of justice.

The two theories of justice most influential in recent years are contractarianism and libertarianism (see page 23). They each build on different perceptions of what justice involves and where primary responsibilities lie. Contractarianism stresses the need to define a reciprocal set of rights and obligations; libertarianism stresses the importance of willingness to pay as the measure of the direction of society's effort in the field of health care. The contractarian stress on reciprocity is a valuable insight in our view. We would not want to endorse the libertarian alternative as it is usually presented, and we note that there is very little support for such an approach in its pure form; but it does bring home the point that the volume and direction of spending is a matter of choice, either at the individual or collective level, so that responsibility for making that choice has to be accepted by some person or group of persons in society.

So far we have not considered the meeting of needs, and this omission is not accidental. To say that needs should be met is not to propose any particular allocation of resources unless we assume that all needs can be met, and this is precisely the assumption that the expansion in health care expenditure calls into question. However,

22

the importance of the principle of satisfying needs is such that some discussion of the idea is called for. To speak of a need is to speak about the necessary condition for achieving a specified or implied end state. If we say that a car needs a replacement distributor in order to run, then we are saying that a necessary condition of the car's

---

TWO CONCEPTIONS OF JUSTICE

Contractarian theory takes seriously the thought that living as a community involves all in sharing benefits and burdens: the point of social contract theory is to provide a model for the agreement whereby all commit themselves to contributing to the common burden in exchange for a share of the common benefit. *Just* social institutions are those that would be agreed upon by the parties to the original contract entered into by individuals forming a society. Clearly, we have not in fact made any such agreement. But modern contractarians – notably John Rawls (1971) in *A Theory of Justice* – suggest that we can derive the substance of the contract that we would agree supposing we had knowledge of human nature and human society but were ignorant of our own position in society. Thus the contract will not reflect selfish desires to establish the kinds of social institutions which favour one group against others. One specific application of Rawls's theory to health care is that of Norman Daniels (1985) in *Just Health Care*. He suggests that one of the principles of justice which would be chosen in the original position is that of equality of opportunity. Since poor health impedes individuals' pursuit of opportunities, in a just society there would be social provision of a level of health care which would restore to sick individuals the range of opportunity that, given their particular range of skills and talents, they would have had if they were healthy.

Libertarian theories of justice take a quite different view of social responsibilities. These theories take as fundamental a very strong conception of individual human rights, including property rights. Each individual has exclusive right to all property legitimately acquired: acquired, that is, without recourse to force or fraud. It is clear, then, that there can be no obligation to contribute any personal property to the general good, whether for the provision of health care or anything else. All health care must be purchased in the free market, whether by direct payment or by private insurance. Libertarian theory has the clear advantage of avoiding the 'bottomless pit' problem. When all health care is provided on an individual willingness to pay basis, there is not the problem of having to decide centrally what level is adequate.

running is the new distributor; without this item the car will not be able to function as it was designed. When applied to human beings the concept of health needs serves to indicate a necessary condition for achieving health. The problem of deciding on the nature of needs is largely a problem of deciding what health might mean, ranging from the World Health Organization's aim of complete mental, physical and social well-being to the minimal conception of health as absence of pain, distress or bodily malfunction.

Fortunately, for our purposes, we do not need to explain what we understand by health. We accept that there are competing and incompatible specifications. We merely assert that however health is defined there are inevitably problems of resource allocation when seeking to meet need in the world as we know it. Even minimalist definitions of health are likely to run up against the problem of resources in the application of the principle of reducing health needs. By the same token, more expansive definitions will also reach limits. It follows from this that the injunction to meet health needs will not be sufficient to guide policy-makers in their task of allocating resources.

Is there anything to be gained in specifying values in the abstract? Not, we think, if people agree in their judgments. But when judgments clash, a set of shared concepts allows the protagonists to move into a larger intellectual space. Disputants who recognise that their own and their opponents' specific judgments presuppose assent to more abstract ideas about, say, the moral limits of markets, or duties to future generations or to the vulnerable, must surely be more able to argue fruitfully than those who do not. They will be able, for example, to identify and control for vested interests, to reach more profound agreement than is yielded by merely weighing the power behind such interests, and to justify their agreed decisions and their compromises to a broader public.

CHAPTER 4

Spending and Political Choice

Health spending is politically controversial; and just as truth is said to be the first casualty of war, so accuracy and impartiality are the first casualties of political campaigns. Nowhere is this more true than with health spending. The total volume of spending on the NHS is an important item of political debate, and as such it has all the characteristics of an ideal weapon of political campaigning. The figure for total spending is made up of diverse elements, and so there is room for endless argument about its different components. The definition of the figure is usually unclear, so by suitable persuasive redefinition, all sides to a debate can usually provide some putative statistical support for their position. Total spending in one year can be compared to total spending in previous years. Therefore, governments can point to increases and oppositions can claim how much more they would have done. And interest groups, either from the supply side or from the numerous groups concerned with the welfare of particular patients, have constant reason for saying that not enough is being spent in particular areas or on particular specialisms. By contrast with the debate on health care spending, the tower of Babel must have been a peaceful place.

Yet no serious discussion of the ethics of resource allocation in the health care system can ignore the problem of how resources are allocated towards the provision of health care as distinct from other goods, especially in a system that is as highly centralised and politically prominent as the NHS. Other countries, like the Federal Republic of Germany, which spend a much higher proportion of their national income on health care, manage to diffuse this particular political controversy through the decentralised nature of their administrative system. In the UK, health care planning is highly centralised and the NHS has to compete with other public expenditure programmes for its share of available public resources. Our study needs to examine the terms in which public legitimacy for levels of public spending on health care can be achieved. In this chapter, therefore, we look at trends over time in expenditure on health in the UK and abroad, and the procedures by which the relevant decisions are taken.

THE NATURE OF HEALTH CARE SPENDING

In all developed countries, governments have accepted responsibility for ensuring that all their citizens have access to some level of health care. This responsibility has been exercised either through direct provision or through financial support. For a variety of reasons, governments have felt the need to control the way in which health care is provided. Unlike other markets, there is usually a considerable imbalance of information between provider and patient, so it is difficult for patients to compare alternatives in the light of experience. To ensure that practitioners do not abuse the power that medical knowledge gives them, entry into the medical profession is usually more or less directly controlled by government. Health care costs often have a 'catastrophic' character coming in large amounts at particular times in a person's life. It is, of course, possible to insure against these costs, but this option will not be available for some individuals, either because they are unable to afford to insure sufficiently for their condition or because they fall into a high risk group and therefore experience discrimination in the way the premiums will be loaded.

Health care revenue and expenditure have therefore become a public matter. The widespread acceptance of this responsibility has been followed by a period in which health care expenditure has grown rapidly in all developed countries. In particular, health care expenditure has grown not only in absolute terms, so that the average citizen of an Organisation for Economic Cooperation and Development (OECD) country now spends a higher amount than he or she would have done 25 years ago, but has also grown in relative terms, so that the average citizen pays a higher proportion of his or her income than would have been true 25 years ago. The quantitative importance of this fact is illustrated in Table 1 (page 27) which gives the elasticity of health expenditures for OECD countries, indicating, that is to say, the growth in health care spending relative to the growth in national income. In all OECD countries we find that as income grows so does health expenditure, and with only two exceptions, Austria and Australia, at a higher rate than income.

The tendency for health care spending to rise as a proportion of national income over time is not an unvarying feature of health care spending, but it is usual. For example, UK health spending as a proportion of GDP dropped between 1981 and 1985 from 6.0 per cent to 5.7 per cent (Schieber and Poullier, 1987, page 108). However, these fluctuations are usually temporary, reflecting recessionary factors in the economy at large which cause spending to grow more slowly

**Table 1   Real elasticities of total health expenditures to gross
domestic product (GDP) 1960–1985**

Australia	1.0	Italy	2.3
Austria	0.9	Japan	1.5
Belgium	1.9	Netherlands	1.4
Canada	1.7	Norway	1.7
Denmark	1.8	Portugal	1.7
Finland	1.9	Spain	2.0
France	2.1	Sweden	3.0
Germany	1.5	Switzerland	2.1
Greece	1.7	United Kingdom	2.2
Ireland	2.4	United States	2.3
Mean	1.9		

Source: Schieber and Poullier, 1987, exhibit 5, page 111.

than the underlying trend. The general movement is steadily
upward. For example, in 1960 the UK spent only 3.9 per cent of its
GDP on health care compared to the 6 per cent or so that obtained in
the 1980s.

The explanations for this growth in proportionate expenditure
have been various. Since salaries usually occupy a significant place in
health spending, absorbing over 70 per cent of expenditure, some
analysts have drawn attention to the 'relative price effect'. This states
that the relative prices of goods and services will rise when it is
difficult to obtain productivity gains by such means as substituting
capital for labour. Since health care tends to be labour intensive, we
might expect the relative price effect to operate with some force.
Moreover, when new pieces of capital equipment are introduced into
health care, they are not always labour saving; they can increase the
demand, for example, for nursing time and create new opportunities
for extra work rather than economising on existing work. Finally,
demographic changes are often said to cause rising expenditure,
particularly with the aging of the population.

There is much controversy about the extent to which any one of
these explanations accounts for the observed trends. Fortunately, for
our purposes, we do not have to come to a judgment about which
explanation is likely to be correct. All we need to do is to indicate
what conclusions might be drawn from the observed trends. The
first point to note is that there is no reason to hold that any particular
rate of growth in health care spending is the inevitable consequence

27

of economic and population trends. As Table 1 shows, the rates of growth vary from country to country indicating that institutional and other specific factors will be at work. Political decisions and policy innovations also can make a difference. The most striking example of this point is to be found in the experience of Canada during the 1970s which managed to restrain growth in the proportion of national income going towards health care by its newly established system of financing. Canada centralised health care insurance and used the monopsonistic powers of the public insurance fund to hold down the growth in providers' salaries (Evans, 1982). The point can be generalised. Analysis of trends in health care spending suggest that centralised systems of finance are somewhat better at containing the growth than are decentralised systems. Political decision-makers have an element of constitutional choice in the government of health systems and therefore can choose to affect the overall level of spending.

To look at the UK's spending in the context of other countries, Table 2 (page 29) provides sufficient evidence to illustrate the salient points. By international standards the United Kingdom spends a lower proportion of its income on health care than most other developed economies. But to ascertain the real difference between resources going into health care is difficult. Much depends, for example, on the relative salaries of professional personnel in the different societies. The detailed comparisons that exist, however, suggest that the published statistics indicate real differences in the effort and resources that societies are willing to devote to health care. For example, Aaron and Schwartz (1984, page 140) estimate that the United States in 1978 spent nearly twice as much as Britain on hospital care per capita, *after allowing for the pay superiority of US medical personnel and the costs of administration, construction and research*. In other words, the differences in health spending that cross-national published statistics report are representative of different implicit decisions in differing societies about the relative priority to be given to health care.

The second point to make about the growth in spending is that it does not have a straightforward relationship to improvements in health. Spending more on the health care system is not obviously the best way of improving a nation's health status. However, it may be worth noting some significant qualifications to this statement. The analysis of the relationship between spending and health status has usually taken age-specific mortality as the measure of health. This is clearly only an imperfect proxy for health, and so there may simply be a bias in the data that are used to test for the relationship. The

28

Table 2   Health care spending as a percentage of gross domestic product (GDP) 1985

	Public	Total
Australia	5.6	7.6
Austria	5.4	7.9
Belgium	5.6	7.3
Canada	6.5	8.6
Denmark	5.2	6.2
Finland	5.6	7.3
France	6.7	9.4
West Germany	6.3	8.1
Greece	4.1	4.2
Iceland	7.0	8.4
Ireland	7.0	8.0
Italy	6.2	7.4
Japan	4.8	6.6
Netherlands	6.6	8.3
Norway	6.3	6.6
Portugal	4.1	5.7
Spain	4.3	6.0
Sweden	8.4	9.3
Switzerland	5.4	7.9
United Kingdom	5.2	5.7
United States	4.4	10.8

Source: Schieber and Poullier, 1987, Exhibits 2 and 3.

relationship is usually also examined at one point in time, so that current spending is associated with current health costs. This ignores the possibility of cumulative effects in the sense that the pace of improvement may be influenced by specific policy initiatives and the funding to support them. For example, Maxwell (1981, page 57) has pointed out that in terms of infant mortality, the UK has slipped down the international league table in recent years when the incremental funding available for development has been less than in many other countries. Hence there may be an underlying relationship between spending and health status, but it will be masked by a number of other factors that also affect health.

The third point to note arises from the second. One of the reasons why it is difficult to observe a relationship between spending and health status is that there is little information about the activities and organisation of health care providers. It is difficult to identify which activities are expensive and which are cheap, and it is difficult to

29

piece together the fragmentary data that do exist. Moreover, even if there were more activity data available, it would be necessary to relate that information to data about the relative effectiveness of different types of clinical procedure. This latter type of data is not available in any systematic form.

Despite the increases in spending that have taken place in the last 25 years, there is still a great deal of public disquiet about current and projected levels of services. The British social attitudes surveys (Jowell, Witherspoon and Brook, 1987, pages 6–7) report a strong and persistent willingness on the part of respondents to have more spent on the NHS, even at the cost of increased taxes (see also, *The Health Services Journal*, 1987, pages 382–83). Other sources of evidence are consistent with these results. However, here again we must be cautious. Since health care spending rises with national income we should expect the UK to spend relatively little given its comparative national income. Moreover, the centralised nature of the UK system will also reduce the proportion that is spent, so that putting both of these factors together we cannot simply assume that the UK is drastically out of international line. To improve policy in the allocation of health care means improving decisions about resources, and this cannot be done simply by assuming a mechanical relationship between aggregates in the national income tables.

Improving decisions requires some familiarity with the way that decisions are made in practice. It might seem a relatively simple matter merely to describe what happens, but in fact we shall touch on a number of issues that are the subject of much controversy. For example, political scientists have spilt much ink over the relative power of the Prime Minister and Cabinet in the UK's system of government. Even questions of description necessarily involve appraisal of various kinds about matters about which it is difficult to obtain firm evidence.

THE PUBLIC EXPENDITURE CYCLE

The set of decisions that fix the terms and limits for all government spending involves deciding how much money to spend on health care in total against other calls on the national or government budget. Constitutionally this is a decision sanctioned by Parliament, but the structure of that decision is determined by a complex interaction between spending ministries, the Treasury and members of the Cabinet. In January of each year the Treasury writes to departments setting out the assumptions they should use in drawing up their plans for future spending. As one of these spending departments, the

DHSS then prepares its spending plans for three years ahead, negotiating on a bilateral basis with the Treasury about details. Within this process political bargaining is of central importance. Individual spending ministers submit bids to the Chief Secretary of the Treasury, usually by the end of May. The Chief Secretary reports to the Cabinet on the overall position, seeks agreement for a target for total spending and acquires a mandate for negotiations bilaterally with spending ministers. At one time it was common for a team of senior officials to reconcile bids in so far as this was possible, but now resolution of bids between officials in advance of bilaterals between ministers is increasingly uncommon. Thus the political role in decision-making is central, although it is of course supported by officials. Since October 1981 there has been a formal Cabinet Committee, designated as Misc 62 but known as the 'Star Chamber', to deal with those issues that cannot be settled by bilateral bargaining. Decisions are taken by October, and an Autumn Statement is made in early November. The Public Expenditure White Paper covering the next three years is then published in January.

Four points of relevance should be noted about this process. Firstly, strategic bargaining by ministers, on behalf of their departments, is likely to be crucial. Fry (1986, page 96) cites the example of Ian Gow who as Minister threatened resignation in 1984 over the cuts in the housing programme despite his general commitment to economic liberalism. Similarly, the memoirs of both Crossman and Barbara Castle suggest the importance of ministers haggling over their share of the cash. Yet when political necessity calls, the Cabinet can move quickly and coherently. For example, on 23 April 1987 the Cabinet was able to agree to implement in full the recommendations for salary increases for nurses and doctors, granting the Secretary of State for Social Services an extra £396m to help fund the increase (*Independent*, 24 April 1987).

Secondly, the politicisation of the process in recent years has to be seen in the context of the government's overall objective of controlling public expenditure and reducing it as a proportion of national income. The effect of this is to make the system less incrementalist than once it was. At one time the best guide to the future development of a programme was its recent past. Now there is a tendency for programmes to diverge in terms of the underlying trend, depending upon their political importance. Thus, in recent years, the rapid reduction of spending in the housing programme has clearly signalled a political judgment about its place in the overall balance of public spending. Naturally previous commitments still

31

constrain present spending, particularly in an area like health where employment and service commitments are strong. Equally, however, one should not underestimate the ability to shift spending priorities where there is a political will in the government of the day.

Thirdly, the figures in the Public Expenditure White Paper are now expressed in cash terms. Until 1976, approval of spending plans by department were expressed in volume terms, so that if inflation increased during the year there would be automatic compensation. Similarly, there is now no increase during the year for unanticipated inflation: the move away from survey prices in 1982 to cash terms meant that spending on health care has to be reduced if inflation turns out to be unexpectedly high.

Fourthly, in all this process Parliament has only a limited role, despite its constitutional responsibility for scrutinising the raising and spending of taxes. There are several factors that work together to push Parliament to the sidelines. Party discipline in the House of Commons is strong, particularly over matters involving public expenditure. Select committees, which can produce cross-bench reports that are highly critical of government, have only limited powers of scrutiny, investigation and examination, and the government may, in any case, choose to defer debates on particular reports. And it is difficult to disentangle issues that are treated together: for example, the Budget which sets the tax rates determines the overall level of public expenditure as a package, without any parliamentary discussion of the effects of marginal changes on particular programmes.

EXPENDITURE WITHIN THE HEALTH CARE SYSTEM

Once it has been agreed what spending is to be allowed for the health programme, the DHSS has responsibility in England for allocating spending between the regional health authorities. We return later to primary care, where expenditure has not been so tightly controlled.

The first stage in the process of distribution is the calculation of the 'target' allocations to the regional health authorities by the Resource Allocation Working Party (RAWP) formula. However, the actual decisions about allocations and the pacing of the exercise is determined by ministers. The RAWP formula has been the basis for both capital and revenue allocations since 1977–78. Its most crucial feature is the attempt to move away from historic-based allocations ('what they had last year plus a bit more' if it could be afforded) to a system that finances authorities according to a rough estimate of relative need. The estimate of relative need is rough because the information needed to refine the formula is simply not available. For example, the present formula is population based, makes adjustments for differences of age and sex, and takes into account standardised mortality, but it contains no information on morbidity. However, as a rough estimate RAWP does seek to equalise (relative to estimated need) the allocations to health authorities that have historically been characterised by marked and arbitrary inequalities. A feature to be noted about RAWP, however, is that its intention is not to equalise service use, but merely the financial allocation to health authorities. Service use and provision is a matter that is explicitly regarded as being within the remit of health authorities. The principle of RAWP is that no health authority should be penalised merely by having an allocation that is less than another authority with like circumstances.

A further feature of the allocation to health authorities is the use of the cost improvement programme (CIP). Each health authority is expected to incorporate within its two year planning programme a set of measures aimed at releasing cash or manpower used in providing a service, either by obtaining the same output for fewer resources or by increasing output at a faster rate than input. The contribution of CIPs to resource allocation has been quite significant: in 1984/85 they yielded 1.1 per cent and in 1985/86 they yielded 1.4 per cent of the total amount of current spending. In 1986/87 the planned cash saving amounted to £158m (Robinson and Judge, 1987, page 6). Health authorities are allowed to retain these savings and they have been used to fund such items as the shortfall in pay awards.

The allocation from regions to districts produces yet another level of decision-making and allocation. Unlike the allocation to regions, there is no set formula that regions are expected to follow in making their allocations to districts. However, in practice, regions have sought to pursue the same policies within their scope of authority as governments have between regions, so that on top of the RAWP redistribution there is also a redistribution within regions. The scale of this process should not be underestimated. One estimate suggests, for example, that two-thirds of the redistribution currently taking place is occurring within the regions rather than as a direct consequence of RAWP at the regional level.

Once at district level the funds have then to be allocated to the units. It is at this final level that the influence of the medical profession implicit in the running of the NHS becomes most obvious. The processes involved are piecemeal and individual. Consultants can increase or decrease their consumption of resources by acts that, although trivial in themselves, can amount to something that is significant – for example, the rate at which they refer patients to x-ray or other forms of diagnostic test. Moreover, resource allocation takes place within a structure of professional authority that is collegial in character, leading two seasoned US observers to describe the British hospital as 'a quasi-feudal enterprise' (Aaron and Schwartz, 1984, page 20). Since consultants rarely move from one post to another, they have a strong incentive to maintain good working relationships with their peers by not arguing about the manner in which the available resources are to be distributed. At a minimum, this takes the form of not publicly decrying anybody else's bid for resources. In consequence, health authorities and their managers are constrained to plan only at the margins of future expenditure, and there is a continual tension between the desire for change and the consultants' inclination to the status quo. In this context the radical approach of Riverside DHA described earlier is rare.

The allocation of funds for primary care currently operates on quite different principles. Apart from their operating budgets, family practitioner committees have not been cash limited, although the Treasury agrees the DHSS's estimate of the costs of the relevant services. The Treasury seeks to estimate costs on this side of the service, and the Department can influence manpower numbers and negotiate contractual terms. But at the end of the day what emerges at the bottom line of the expenditure statement is what is demanded within the system by patients initiating health care episodes and doctors' prescribing treatment regimes. The lack of financial control on the primary care side, contrasting so markedly with the stringent control of health authorities, reflects both the status of general practitioners as independent contractors operating their small business enterprises within negotiated terms and conditions of service and the hitherto relatively low proportion of total health care spending they have consumed.

Patients and potential patients have the most marginal role within this system. Lay people are of course involved in the political decisions on what should be spent, and what the system's priorities should be, just as they are involved on regional and district health authorities. And the whole of government is accountable to the electorate through the democratic process. But once resources reach unit level there is little direct link between patient preferences and resource allocation. In the absence of a price mechanism, consumers have no ready device for signalling to those who treat them what they value and what they find onerous. Nor is there a large insurance market offering differing types of contracts for care to those willing to pay different amounts. In these circumstances, patient priorities have to be mediated through the perceptions of managers and clinicians, through official consultative channels such as community health councils, or through politicians.

SOME GENERAL CHARACTERISTICS OF THE SYSTEM

Although our description of the system has been sketchy we hope it serves to underline and give some substance to the generalisations we now wish to make about the character of decision-making within the NHS. There are four features in particular that we think are important.

Firstly, there are impressive mechanisms of financial accountability built into the system. Most health authorities in most years manage to balance their books whatever the level of cost pressure to which they are subject. However, the control exercised through this system of accountability is over personnel and tangible resources, not over the activities of clinicians. Moreover, since the government has squeezed resources in the NHS, so that there is little 'give', clinical activity has become an important factor in health care costs. It has been argued (Aaron and Schwartz, 1984) that the system of budgeting in Britain slows down the rate of clinical innovation. Although this may be true of those procedures that require additional physical resources before they can be started (the purchase of expensive diagnostic equipment, for example) it is not generally true when we turn to the broad spectrum of clinical activities. To take one simple example, cranial artery bypass surgery was introduced into the UK and has been practised before adequate evaluation (see *New England Journal of Medicine*, 1987). Clinical autonomy insulates clinicians from accountability about the use of their time and energies whereas it does not insulate them from accountability for the use of resources.

Secondly, the system contains a large capacity for double-talk and even double-think. This can be illustrated by reference to three examples. Pay is the largest component of health care spending, and yet within the cash-limited budgets allocated to health authorities the provision for pay settlements has often been inadequate. Health authorities have therefore been left with the financial consequences of pay bargains between the government and the pay review bodies to which they have not been party. A similar story can be told about allowances for technological improvements. Currently 0.5 per cent per annum is allowed for the costs associated with technological advance, but it is difficult to know what scale of medical advance this figure is supposed to represent. At present the DHSS calculates this

35

figure by estimating the increase in the number of cases arising from technological innovations and combines this figure with estimates in increases in average costs. However, this approach conflates changes in cost arising from technological improvements with increases in the standard of care that more advanced techniques may be expected to bring about. Neither the DHSS nor anyone else is asked to state what is an appropriate standard of care for the expenditure that is incurred (see *Health Care UK*, 1986, page 91). The cost improvement programme also suffers from a similar ambiguity. It is not possible to explain the grounds on which the figures used in the CIPs have been chosen, and it is not difficult to see how cost improvements might actually take the form of cuts in services – a danger against which the National Audit Office has warned (National Audit Office, 1986, pages 9–10). So in these three examples – pay, the costs of technology and supposed cost improvements – it is possible to see a cloud of ambiguity (if not downright dishonesty) that makes political accountability and responsiveness difficult to achieve.

Thirdly, the steady round of annual budgeting has benefits for routine expenditures. But it is slow to respond to crises and in a period of tightening resources it is prone to problems at the margins when delivering services at local level. The initial allocations to districts who were beginning to encounter difficulties with AIDS was an example of sluggish response. An example of problems at the margin is the competition for resources at district level between all the inherited responsibilities and new ministerial priorities which were not fully funded. The pressure in either situation is to put a brave face on things and hope that solutions will be found.

Fourthly, there is no mechanism by which patients, as the ultimate users of the service, can effectively influence decisions about the volume and quality of care that is to be delivered. The conventional wisdom is that the effects of this are noticed on the amenity rather than the medical side of the NHS, hence the popular explanations of why people are prepared to pay to make use of the private sector. But the distinction between amenity and medical need is not always easy to draw, as the example of waiting list times goes to show.

IMPLICATIONS FOR THE STUDY OF ETHICS

We cannot expect to draw any ethical conclusions simply by describing how decisions are made. Nonetheless, we can draw out the lessons about the type of decision-making mechanism involved in allocating resources in the NHS, and the constraints that exist on choices. Although our survey of decision-making has been brief, we hope that it has highlighted certain important features, most notably the amount of discretion that is built into the system. At the level of allocating resources to the health system as a whole, there is clearly a large amount of discretion, especially if we focus not upon a single year but upon the trends and pattern of expenditure that may be built up over a number of years. Although regions and districts operate within tight budgetary restraints, it is clear that at these levels also there is discretion, as the example of regional RAWPs goes to show. Finally, at the level of the unit and ward, clinicians have considerable discretion as far as the use of resources is concerned. The first implication that follows from these observations is the need for a strong internalised sense of responsibility in relation to the task of allocating resources. This responsibility extends beyond the customary business of discharging one's obligations conscientiously and with integrity. It includes also the obligation to think critically about the duties one is being asked to perform and the principles upon which one is obliged to act. In our opinion it is especially necessary to introduce this 'critical' morality alongside customary morality in a health service in which the power of patients to alter or affect policy is limited. Without the devices of a price mechanism, strong ties of accountability or patient representation on policy-making bodies, the assessment of the quality of care that a patient receives can too easily be assumed to be satisfactory without proper evidence or investigation.

In saying this we do not mean to weaken the ties of responsibility that exist between a particular patient and a named doctor. It is customary within our health care system for responsibility, including responsibility for the use of resources, to be individualised in this way. We are suggesting that there is an additional responsibility that arises for all those engaged in the delivery of health services to appraise critically the use and allocation of resources in the system as a whole. There are, and always will be, marked differences between responsibilities for resource allocation exercised by different people, measured in financial terms, the numbers of people affected, and so on. There is, however, a responsibility on all those involved in affecting the allocation to reflect upon the principles and processes involved, and to make a constructive contribution to improvement. This is especially important since, in our description of political and administrative decision-making, we have highlighted the arbitrary elements and the processes of bargaining that are likely to be inconsistent with pursuit of the common good.

Resource allocation is a subtle process that changes its character at different levels and over time. Financial accountability, control and cost containment, even when successful, still have defects. And this too argues for an internalised sense of responsibility to which ethical principle will be relevant. The problem is to bring to bear ethical principles on the circumstances within which hard choices have to be made.

CHAPTER 5

Accountability

Let us review where we have arrived in the argument. We began with a series of examples that prompted a concern with ethical issues in the allocation of health care resources. The nature of the choices that confront health care practitioners and planners meant that it was inadequate merely to think about problems at a high level of generality. Detailed thinking was needed about the ethical principles that should inform political, administrative and medical choices to avoid the danger that expediency and the assertion of mere power would substitute for justifiable action. In applying these principles we should be sensitive to the differences in ethical perspective that arise at national, institutional and individual levels. The considerations that should weigh in the choices of politicians and civil servants will not always be those that should weigh with planners or clinicians. What we can hope to do, however, is to identify a common vocabulary of discourse within which priorities may be discussed. To this end we identified four principles that were relevant when seeking to avoid expediency: autonomy, beneficence, non-maleficence and justice. The task of an ethics of health care resource allocation is to bring these principles to bear upon the world of practice. That world is complex and conditioned by the force of past practice and institutional constraints, but we should not allow the complexity and the sense that change is difficult to provide an excuse for failing to apply the principles of critical morality to one of our most important public services.

At this point, however, we face a dilemma. Many will urge that there is no 'right answer' to the problems we are discussing. The moral pluralism that characterises our society means that individuals and groups will differ in their response to these questions. These differences will range over all the issues central to the current debate: the scope of public responsibility for the care of the sick; the relative importance of justice and efficiency in the use of resources; the authority that clinicians or managers should have to make hard choices; the competing claims of other demands on the national purse; the priority that is to be given to different client-groups; and so on. The fundamental point about these differences is not that they are inevitable, but that they all represent points of view that may

39

properly be held by reasonable persons concerned to promote and advance the public interest. Faced with a multiplicity of viewpoints it is tempting to say that nothing of general value can be asserted. All that we are left with is a diversity of views and the government has to make decisions as best it can, recognising that there will always be viewpoints and interests that cannot be fully acknowledged, weighed and reflected in its policy: to decide is to reject one alternative in favour of another. From this perspective, ethical reasoning about such matters is not so much naive as merely one-sided in failing to recognise that governments and public decision-makers must reconcile a variety of viewpoints.

Is there anything that can be said in reply to this charge? We believe that there is and that an understanding of what more is involved in the tasks of governing and administering a national health service is central to coping with the issues raised in the ethics of resource allocation. In essence the claim we are making is simple. It is that a public obligation is held in trust by the government on behalf of the members of society and therefore the government owes a duty to society to ensure that it manages that trust responsibly. The discharge of that duty involves appeal to the values and principles contained in a common civic culture. Part of the duty involves ensuring that resources are obtained and used in a justifiable manner. Unless decisions can be justified by appeal to the values of a civic culture, the trust has not been discharged responsibly. If the burden of justification has been discharged, then individuals and groups of citizens may prefer that some other decisions had been made, but they cannot complain that the public authorities have acted irresponsibly. In other words, the responsible discharge of the public trust that is implicit in the National Health Service involves government, administrators and managers convincing health providers, the public and patients in debate, not merely engaging in the unprincipled exercise of political power. All involved in making decisions are therefore accountable for the discharge of their responsibilities, and no decision on resource allocation is justifiable unless it can be rendered accountable.

By accountability in this context we are principally referring to a moral notion rather than a legal or constitutional concept. As Nairne (1984, page 34) emphasised, the constitutional accountability of the NHS flows upward to the DHSS and then it is discharged before Parliament and the appropriate select committees. Accountability in this sense is the obligation to answer questions, to explain the purpose of policy and to provide an account of the way in which expenditure and resources are managed. There is a broader notion of accountability, however. In this broader concept of accountability what is being sought is an explanation of the grounds on which a policy is being pursued, not only through the formal mechanisms of parliamentary control, but also as part of a more general public dialogue between all those with an interest in the matter. In this dialogue it is essential that the government and other parties strive for an honest understanding of the viewpoints of others involved.

The principal accountabilities in this context are between physician, or other health care professionals, and patient; between health authorities and the populations they serve; and between the NHS as a whole and central government on behalf of the nation. Of course there are other accountabilities too: among colleagues; within a profession; between employee and employer; and from health authorities via RHAs and the NHS Management Board to ministers. Indeed this last line of accountability is sufficiently firm that some would argue it takes precedence over local accountability, although chairmen and members of health authorities and district general managers typically feel a strong pull in both directions.

The essential concept of accountability is that the person who is accountable acts on behalf of others and owes it to those others to carry out their wishes and give a proper record of his or her stewardship. It goes much further than financial accountability, already mentioned in the context of NHS financing. If accountability is real rather than nominal, then a major factor in resource allocation decisions should be the wishes of patients (when they concern choices about their own treatment and when their choices do not threaten the interest of others), the local community (as an expression of local needs and priorities) and the nation (in determining the range and overall funding of the services, and formulating national priorities). These levels of accountability correspond to what we have called the individual, institutional and national levels of resource allocation.

We are not saying that there is an automatic correspondence of interest or viewpoint between these different levels. However, such differences as there are will not be reconciled in any way unless there is an attempt by government to set out and defend the principles upon which decisions are made, which may then be subject to public scrutiny. Where conflicts exist, it is necessary that those involved understand why there are competing claims and why their claim has received the priority it has. This can only be accomplished if there is a conscious attempt to draw upon the moral resources of a civic culture. In our civic culture, that essentially means being able to account for and justify decisions in terms of the principles of

41

autonomy, non-maleficence, beneficence and justice. In the present context the most important of these is the principle of autonomy.

AUTONOMY AND ACCOUNTABILITY

The principle of autonomy demands that people should respect each other's 'space' for thought, intention and action, as long as the individual concerned is capable of exercising deliberated choice and does not threaten the autonomy of others. This must imply, for example, that competent patients should normally decide what treatment they do *not* want, or what risks they prefer not to take based on the best advice their physicians can give them. Only in rare instances, such as dangerous or infectious patients, might these wishes be overridden. Equally the principle provides the basis for clinical autonomy, within the bounds of the patient's wishes, resource constraints, a concern for effectiveness, reasonable policy guidelines, and the norms of acceptable professional practice. Nor should physicians be compelled to act against their conscience, but in that case they may well have a duty to help the patient obtain help elsewhere.

Similarly, choices about the use of scarce resources are ultimately the responsibility of those who represent the public – for example, as members of health authorities or in central government. At the local level, health authority members need advice from the health care professions and from managers about the implications of their decisions, but they are responsible for determining the public interest and that is how their choices should be explained and justified. That authority members find such choices hard is an argument for helping them to develop their capability to discharge them, not for taking them covertly. Health authorities do not find this easy – general managers are still trying to improve ways of reconciling conflicting pressures and interest groups. Moreover, the existence of RHAs as well as DHAs complicates the situation since there can arise an uncertainty about where responsibility for initiatives and savings resides. But just as surely as it is the physician's duty to let the patient decide, with the best advice and support he or she can give, so it is up to the general manager to explain the real choices to the health authority. A similar duty lies between the NHS Management Board and ministers, and the national choices ought to be clearly explained to the nation rather than taken in secret. The extract from the Crossman Diaries on pages 15–16 illustrates the power struggles between spending ministries and the Treasury that provide an unsatisfactory basis on which to make decisions. There is therefore a need to ensure that this duty of explanation is discharged. All this may sound obvious but it is often overlooked. If it were heeded it would help, since the most difficult resource allocation decisions are not purely technical but depend, in the end, on judgment. Whose judgment should be preferred to that of those who are most affected?

In any decision about resource allocation it is necessary to specify:

1   the sphere or community of interests served by the decision, including that of providers;

2   the people within that sphere who will be affected; and

3   the accuracy with which a service can be directed at those of the target group who are considered most in need of it.

This may be expressed in another way: any person responsible for resources should have a defined community sphere (or spheres) of responsibility and should strive to become aware of the people within that sphere towards whom the resources are being, or will be, directed or withheld.

It will help to make this point of view clearer if we spell out some examples of what may be involved. Thus, at the level of individual decision making, the concept that the patient presenting is the only patient that matters is too narrow. Since resources used for one patient will not be available for another, the clinician may have to make a decision that involves considerations wider than that of individual need. An example of how hard these choices can be was provided by our first example, where a renal unit was simply unable to accept a patient onto its dialysis programme because to do so would risk jeopardising a resource for others. Similarly, at an institutional level it is not in order simply to press vigorously for one's own specialism without thought for the consequences for others, thereby abnegating responsibility by insisting that the process of decision-making adjudicates between rival claims.

At every level of management in the allocation of resources, conflicts are likely to arise because the individuals concerned see their responsibilities as directed towards different populations of health care recipients. These conflicts may arise also within the individual because different roles require different responsibilities. The district general manager's responsibility for meeting district service needs may, for example, appear to clash with the consultant's belief that his or her special interest constitutes an unrecognised regional or national specialty serving people from outside the district. And, of course, the consultant feels obliged to provide the best possible service to each patient he or she is asked to treat. Furthermore, the consultant's teaching duties and research interests cannot readily be subsumed under a purely district role. The ward nurse is responsible for the patients under her care on the ward but the doctor responsible for admissions is motivated also by awareness of the people not on the ward for whom urgent admission is or may be needed. The phlebotomist (the person who takes blood) has to face a queue waiting for blood tests and is reluctant to take on the perceived hazard and extra burden of tests for AIDS; the senior pathology technician, however, is keen to provide a good service to potential AIDS sufferers and to enhance the status of the non-medical staff in the department; asking doctors to take blood in such cases will undermine these aims. And so on.

At the national level it is particularly important to recognise the clash of interests and to acknowledge accountability in seeking to exercise responsibility wisely for the control of health care resources. The control of costs involves placing burdens potentially on three groups of people: providers, patients and citizens who are, ultimately, financers of the system. None of these groups has automatic priority over the other when considering claims on resources. Governments should therefore strive to ensure that the decisions they take can be defended in public debate and should be able to withstand critical scrutiny.

STRENGTHENING ACCOUNTABILITY

Some useful ideas to strengthen accountability include the following:

1 *The concept of an implicit covenant* Contracts need not be formal or written, as long as people have a clear mutual expectation and stick by it. The idea of covenant goes beyond the narrow legal definition of contract to one of mutual commitment and mutual trust. Thus, for example, patients are entitled to trust their doctors and to receive an explanation and an apology if mistakes are made. At the institutional and national levels, financial allocation ought at last to be based on a clear, if informal, agreement on what is expected for the money and what cannot reasonably be financed within it. A public dialogue on these lines at national level should increase public understanding.

2 *The importance of due process* People who disagree with a decision will find it easier to accept if it was taken in the appropriate forum in an explicable, recognised way. For example, the decision whether to operate on a baby with Down's syndrome or on an

unconscious patient cannot be decided by the patient, and people may disagree profoundly as to what is the right decision. In such a situation it helps to have a process agreed in advance where different views can be heard and a decision reached. At the health authority level, to take a different example, people are likely to disagree about which services should be expanded or reduced in conditions of severe resource constraint. Again, those concerned will find it easier to live with the choices made, even if they do not like them, if they understand and respect the way in which the decisions were reached. Principled judgment between competing claims is required by justice, and agreement about the process of achieving such principled judgment allows justice to be seen to be done.

3 *The need for honesty* Honesty and avoidance of deceit are corollaries of the principle of respect for autonomy. One generic example in which honesty may be lost is in the dealings between managers and clinicians. It is tempting on both sides to distort the argument, or cast the evidence favourably in what is thought to be a good cause. But, once found out, the culprits forfeit any right to respect. This means that information obtained during the course of one's activity needs to be shared responsibly with those with whom one is in negotiation. Clinicians should avoid seeking to distort claims and managers should seek to state the choices openly and indicate why they have a preferred course of action. The case for honesty here rests not simply with the danger of being found out, but in a whole attitude of mind. If participants in the process do not strive to be honest, they are unlikely to strive to make the best decisions in the public interest.

4 *The need to enhance decision-making space* Shortage of resources has challenged some of the interpretations of the notion of clinical autonomy. At one extreme it has been based on the concept that the actions of a professional can be circumscribed and questioned only, if at all, by peer group challenge or the law. Thus, as a consequence, a doctor should not consider resources at all when deciding how to treat his patients. This view has been heard less often of late and BMA guidance on ethics now acknowledges the need for clinicians to work within a reasonable resource framework. This tighter definition of autonomy preserves the doctor's clinical discretion as to how he handles treatment within the given framework. We believe that space must be preserved for clinicians to use their discretion, but that they are obligated first to their patients and potential patients, second to their colleagues and third to their *de facto* employers.

At the institutional level one cannot expect managers to use their initiative if they are kept on a very tight rein and their confidence undermined. They should be working very closely with the health authority, consumer organisations, other officials and the medical staff to provide the best possible local service. There is not a hope of leadership from them if they are treated as functionaries, acting under central instructions which often seem bounded by short-term considerations. They should be accorded a similar degree of autonomy as we recognise as crucial for clinicians and should be supported by their health authorities and the NHS Management Board, providing that their actions are reasonable.

5   *Individual and community development*   Exercising choice is the crucial means by which citizens and the community can develop their capacity for responsible action, including the allocation of scarce resources. Advocacy schemes have a place here, in amplifying the voice of those who may for a variety of reasons find it difficult to be heard. Based ultimately on a legal model, these schemes seek to provide agents whose jobs it is to try to understand and express what their clients want. Such schemes have been tried successfully for, among others, people with learning difficulties, people who are mentally ill, and the disadvantaged, including members of ethnic minorities. Moreover, physicians and managers who want public participation to be a reality are going to have to be effective community developers, and will need to enjoy good relations with community health councils, self-help patient groups and many other organisations. It is also worth noting how bad professional and institutional decisions can undermine people's capacity for autonomy.

6   *Health authority development*   Work by Day and Klein (1987) on public accountability in health authorities indicates wide variations in members' confidence about their role. Their sense of their own legitimacy was one important variable and it was thought that it would help if members were elected by the public. Another factor was whether there was a convincing set of measures of performance, reflecting a shared clarity about what the authority was there to do. In the case of health, there was a lot of ambiguity and confusion. This suggests that members' understanding of their role should be increased to prepare them for a stronger part in resource allocation decisions. The other chapters of this book have mainly concentrated on the ethics of resource allocation as though the decisions could be perfected within one person's head. But they cannot. One way or another in a national health service they are in the public domain

where autonomy requires accountability. If we get accountability right, we can enhance autonomy. If we do not, autonomy will not be respected.

7   *The establishment of a body of moral 'case law'*   When clinicians, managers, health authorities and planners are faced with difficult moral choices, it may help if they keep a record of the case, and the grounds on which the final choice was made. By this device they will build up a body of moral case law. Comparing judgments across this body of decisions will help to ensure consistency and promote the virtue of justice; it should also provide material for reflection, learning and an exchange of views about the rightness of the decision. Making moral choices can never be a mechanical matter of applying precedents, but there is scope for developing judgment in relation to difficult cases that are not the subject of immediate practical choice.

The Search for Effectiveness

Accountability requires a civic culture to guide the decisions of those responsible for allocating resources. However, it also requires a large store of information about actual and potential practice. As we have noted previously, there is little information available about the effectiveness and cost of a wide range of clinical procedures. Unless we can differentiate between practices that are worthwhile and those that are not, we have little chance of acting responsibly. This chapter, therefore, examines issues associated with the search for effectiveness.

THE NEED FOR EFFECTIVENESS

'It may seem a strange principle to enunciate as the very first requirement in a hospital that it should do the sick no harm', wrote Florence Nightingale (1863, page iii). In Nightingale's day the sources of harm were to be found in the insanitary conditions under which care was administered and operations performed. Nightingale's mission was to improve conditions so that hospitals performed their intended purpose of contributing to the recovery of the sick. The ultimate source of the problem was to be found in the negligence that allowed insanitary conditions to persist. The strength of character that Nightingale possessed and needed to accomplish her self-appointed task indicates how widespread negligent attitudes were.

However, the need to minimise harm is still with us, and in some ways it is more deeply entrenched in the practice of the modern hospital than it was in Nightingale's day. The problem of avoiding harm nowadays arises from the far greater range and potency of the procedures that are currently practised. They arise, in other words, from the need to ensure that medical procedures are as effective as they are claimed to be.

An example will illustrate the point. Some ten years ago an operation known as radial keratotomy was developed in the Soviet Union in an attempt to find a surgical cure for short-sightedness. The operation can be performed under local anaesthetic, and it involves merely making a few cuts on the surface of the eye. In the United States in particular the operation has become widely used, although doubts about its safety and efficacy remain. About one in ten patients are dissatisfied when examined a year after the operation, mainly because of uncorrected visual acuity or refractive errors, daily fluctuations in vision, or glare. There may well be longer-term complications (Chalmers, 1986, page 156). The example is not an isolated one. Probably a high proportion of those reading this work will have had tonsillectomies when children, an operation that has been subsequently shown to be ineffective for many patients in achieving its stated purposes. The problem of effectiveness is not in itself a problem of expense. Some ineffective procedures may be relatively cheap. The point, however, is that if they do not achieve their intended aims they are a waste of resources in an absolute sense and they violate the principle of non-maleficence on which health care should be based.

There is an interesting difference in our attitudes towards new drugs on the one hand and new surgical procedures on the other. With new drugs we reverse the rules of evidence that we apply to court cases: the drug is presumed guilty until its innocence is proved in controlled trials and surveillance for adverse effects. We carry this presumption to the point where even if the drug shows some benefits it will not be marketed if it also shows harmful effects. No such principle applies in a general way towards surgical or other procedures used within health services. Many procedures are introduced without a systematic effort to investigate their effects. More significantly, perhaps, there can often be considerable pressure from patients to introduce procedures, despite the lack of reliable evidence over effects, in the hope that some good will be done.

The situation therefore is complex. Historically the development of modern medicine has been a battle against the ineffectiveness of traditional procedures within the hospital. Despite the elimination of many procedures that have become discredited, there is absolutely no guarantee that all procedures that are currently in use are effective.

APPLYING THE PRINCIPLE OF EFFECTIVENESS

In its simplest sense, effectiveness means the ability of a procedure to accomplish a given end. However, the boundaries of what is included in the procedure need to be rather carefully thought of, since medical procedures, like any form of technology, comprise not only the hardware and equipment that is needed to accomplish a given task but also the skills and knowledge of those in a position to carry out that task. Hence Cochrane (1972) and others have differentiated efficacy (or impact under ideal conditions) from effectiveness (or impact in normal use). For procedures to be effective in practice, medical and nursing personnel are to be under a professional obligation to acquaint themselves with developments in the subject and generally to keep up to date with developing practice. Collectively each profession also has a duty to subject its practices to disciplined enquiry and to see that the acts of its members meet acceptable standards.

Technological developments also affect the way in which responsibility for achieving effectiveness is divided between medical and associated personnel. In the treatment of kidney patients, for example, responsibility for care will in practice often fall upon nurses, technicians and others. The relationship of ultimate responsibility between a named doctor and a named patient is unaffected by the changing division of labour among medical teams, but the example does provide an instance of the way in which the maintenance of effective treatment requires continuously ensuring that the skills and training of personnel are up to date and that their efforts are coordinated appropriately.

However, simply by virtue of their professional qualifications and expertise, physicians and other health care personnel are not in a sound position to obtain reliable evidence on the effectiveness of a particular technique, unless the health care system as a whole arranges for the scientific testing and evaluation of procedures. It follows from this that a priority of the health care system should be to arrange for the rigorous testing of procedures, if it is to discharge its obligation to use resources wisely and if it is to be in a position to enable medical and nursing personnel to discharge their obligation to act in the best interests of their patients.

To adopt the principle that medical procedures should be tested for their effectiveness is not to dictate the manner in which this testing is to be organised, nor to say anything about the priority that the testing of one procedure is to have over another. Many of the issues involved in the judgment of priorities fall outside the scope of ethical reasoning and are more properly regarded as administrative or scientific matters. However, there is one issue of priority on which we feel we ought to comment, and that is whether all procedures ought to be tested or whether restrictions ought only to be placed on innovation.

Favouring something simply because it is old and established makes little sense. However, we believe that there are some reasons why special restrictions ought to apply to new procedures which do not apply equally to established ones. New procedures are often technologically sophisticated and therefore relatively expensive. The need arises, therefore, to ensure that they yield value for money in the minimal sense of at least doing what is claimed for them, without unforeseen side effects. Established procedures have also withstood some test of experience, even if it is not the systematic test that is involved in a controlled trial. Finally, there are thousands of established procedures that make large demands on resources, either through their high cost-per-case or their high volume. It would be a Herculean task to impose a rational order on the priority for their testing. It would of course make sense to test selected procedures over which doubt arises or where there are strongly divergent views: radical mastectomy provides such an example, as does ECT. Equally it would certainly be sensible in this context to give priority to the testing of particularly expensive procedures that make large demands on resources. But the main priority must be to ensure that the public does not remain the subjects for *uncontrolled* trials of new procedures.

One of the reasons why a concern for effectiveness needs to be taken seriously is that there are many pressures within the policy-making process that are likely to oppose the search for rational evidence about the effects of different technologies. In the United States, the National Center for Health Care Technology, a body concerned with the impartial investigation of medical technologies, was closed after three years following Congressional lobbying by both the American Medical Association and the Health Industry Manufacturers' Association. In the United Kingdom, one source of ineffectiveness has lain in voluntary donations of pieces of equipment to hospitals that have been ill-suited to the circumstances and tasks that the hospital had to accomplish. Quite often there is collusion (none the less dangerous for being well-intentioned) between an ambitious clinician, who wishes to establish a reputation for doing new things, and a public anxious to find new remedies.

The job of seeking for effectiveness is, for a variety of reasons, not one that can simply be left to medical practitioners. To measure effectiveness involves the systematic collection of data that requires specific skills and must normally be part of a team or institutional effort. To do poor studies is worse than useless, not simply because it wastes time and money, but because it may bring discredit on the enquiries of others and miss a crucial opportunity to test authoritatively the impact of some new procedure (as for example through a properly conducted randomly controlled trial). Many practitioners will have competing calls on their time and energies, so for this reason also a corporate initiative will often be needed. More importantly, the measure of effectiveness requires value judgments that medical practitioners are no more privileged to make than anyone else. Once issues concern not simply medical conditions as abstract entities but also quality of life, then the subjective perceptions of present and future patients, as well as the perceptions of relatives and next of kin, become important. Lacking a suitable forum in which perceptions and experience can be pooled, it is hard to go beyond generalised statements to the effect that the duty to search for effectiveness should be widely shared among interested parties.

In the context of this report, the disciplined assessment of therapeutic effectiveness is not going to solve all our problems. At the end of the day, in our judgment, there will be more therapies that offer some genuine (if expensive or marginal) benefit than the NHS can afford. Nevertheless it must be right to remove from contention therapies that do little or no good. We conclude that there are three essentials:

1   To test in a controlled way all new procedures before they are introduced into general use. This is likely to require a sequence of steps: permission to experiment; introduction in a few centres equipped for proper trials; and clearance for more general introduction.

2   To select for equally rigorous testing existing procedures that for various reasons, including their total impact on costs, are priority candidates for evaluation.

3   To ensure that the difficult task of evaluation is done sufficiently well that the resulting evidence provides a sound basis for decisions about the introduction or elimination of competing therapies. Unfortunately the evidence will usually be imperfect, if only because no therapy stands still and because the cure of disease is different in every patient. Science cannot resolve ethical dilemmas, but it should be able to ensure that information that can reasonably be obtained is valid and sound.

EFFECTIVENESS IN PRACTICE

Even if we suppose that procedures used are efficacious in principle, the skill and organisation with which they are put into practice will condition their effectiveness, and hence whether the resources have been well used. The Confidential Enquiry into Perioperative Deaths (CEPOD) reveals how much difference can be made by the proper exercise of skills and organisation in practice. The study was based in three regions and investigated all deaths up to 30 days after the operation over a given period of time. In some respects the results of the enquiry are encouraging: 95 per cent of consultants in anaesthesia and surgery agreed to participate and the overall mortality rate for some half a million operations was only 0.7 per cent. Against this must be set some other points, however. The few consultants who refused to cooperate caused the loss to the study of the review of a substantial proportion of perioperative deaths in their hospitals, and even those who did participate showed little interest in the review of their practice carried out by the assessors in the study team. Forty per cent of general surgeons had neither regular meetings about deaths and complications, nor any arrangements for audit in general (*The Lancet*, 1987, pages 1369–71; Lunn and Devlin, 1987, pages 1384–86). In short, even a general receptiveness to the idea of peer review and audit does not translate in all cases into specific practical measures for its implementation. Two points about ethical responsibility stand out.

Firstly, those involved at the individual level of resource allocation need to ensure that resources are well used, and this must involve taking specific steps to ensure that professional practice is maintained to high standards. There is no excuse for those who both claim the privileges of professional autonomy and mismanage the resources they are allocated. If the CEPOD findings are accurate, there is potential for improvement, and peer review and audit offer a way forward. Secondly, health authorities and managers need to ensure that resources are made available to support a willingness to undertake peer review. This may take the form of clerical and computing resources, or it may involve ensuring that the conditions for effective teamwork exist in hospital. Provision for improvements in practice should not be reserved for the odd 'champion' or enthusiast, but should be incorporated into the routines of typical case management.

CHAPTER 7

The Search for Efficiency

Suppose that as a nation we are spending just the right proportion of our national resources on health care. Suppose that we are allocating financial resources in such a way that there is no arbitrariness between different spending authorities. Suppose further that we have taken steps to ensure that our procedures are effective. Then it might seem that the problems of resource allocation were exhausted. Unfortunately, this would be a mistake. It can be argued that at this point we would face the most serious problems of resource allocation – namely, determining priorities between different persons and patient-groups. Given that we never have sufficient resources to meet all needs, what priority should we give to meeting some medical needs compared to others?

It is clear that the answer to this question depends not only on the seriousness of the needs in question, but also on the relative costs involved in meeting those needs. In other words, it depends upon economic considerations of a very obvious kind. There is a wide-spread view that the economic approach to questions of the allocation of health care resources confuses what should be essentially separate considerations. Clinical judgments should be kept free from economic calculation. In particular, the introduction of economic considerations is thought to create a situation in which the age, class and social usefulness of the patient become relevant to choices about treatment in ways that are precluded by an attitude that focuses exclusively on the clinical condition of the patient. Moreover, these differences of attitude are reinforced by differences of role. Administrators see themselves as primarily concerned with the allocation of resources and clinicians see themselves as concerned with the duties of care and cure. Such issues might be thought to be particularly acute in the NHS in which the primary commitment is to treat patients on the basis of need rather than ability to pay. There is legitimate reason to be concerned about economic techniques if their effect was to reintroduce surreptitiously considerations of social and economic status which it is the intention of the NHS to exclude.

THE ECONOMIC APPROACH

At first sight the conflict between the economic approach to the allocation of resources and the traditional ethic of medical obligation seems stark and uncompromising. The traditional ethic of medical treatment enjoins all those responsible for the care of the sick to do their utmost to effect a cure. The logic of economic calculation is to trade off benefits against costs. The traditional ethic requires that those who care for the sick focus their attention on the specific person in front of them. The logic of economic calculation is to consider the effects of individual decisions on all those who are touched by their consequences. The traditional ethic requires that the maintenance of individual life be given supreme value. The logic of economic calculation is to allow that individuals' lives may be sacrificed in order to achieve a benefit elsewhere. Without prejudice to the question of which stance is to be preferred, it would seem that in this contrast of views we are dealing with sharply differentiated positions.

Putting the matter in this way, however, produces a paradox. Whatever the traditional medical ethic may prescribe it is clear that not even the most conscientious practitioners take its injunctions literally. The absolute commitment to each patient is limited in reality by a whole variety of factors that are not intrinsically related to medical practice. The obligations of contract to others, the ties of colleagues and family and even the need to spend time and energy in maintaining and developing medical expertise for the benefit of future patients all limit the extent to which practitioners devote themselves to any one patient, and it is generally recognised that it is proper that it is so (Williams, undated). Looking at the matter from the patient's point of view it is clear that as potential patients we do not feel it is worthwhile going to any lengths whatsoever to ensure that we have the most extensive medical care when we are sick. Collectively we spend less on the NHS than most other developed countries spend on their medical care, and even among the high spending countries like Sweden and the USA there are calls to spend more. Quite apart from money, we can easily conceive situations in which more medical intervention is the last thing we would want. What we find proper and acceptable is at variance with the absolutist prescriptions of the traditional medical ethic, and involves quite properly an economic component.

To speak strictly, the economic approach is not one method of making decisions, but a family of methods each of which accepts the need to think in terms of relative priorities. When thinking about the

55

problems and difficulties raised by the economic approach, we have found it useful to focus on the work of Professor Alan Williams, who has sought systematically to develop the logic of this form of analysis (Williams, 1985, 1986). In particular, Professor Williams advocates the use of 'quality adjusted life years', or QALYs for short, as a way of assessing the relative value of different clinical and preventive procedures. In assessing the economic approach to the valuation of human life, therefore, we focus on the issue of QALYs, their construction and their meaning.

The essence of the QALY approach is to say that in making an allocation of resources in the health care system we ought properly to think both of the costs and the benefits that alternative clinical and preventive procedures involve. (For the sake of simplicity we shall talk about clinical procedures only, although, as we shall see, one of the great merits of the QALY approach is that it enables us to compare clinical and non-clinical procedures in terms of their efficiency.) The costs comprise the time and effort as well as the material resources that are deployed in using any particular procedure. The calculation includes costs imposed on patients and their families, as well as those incurred by providers. There are, of course, great difficulties in measuring these costs, and in any particular case it is necessary that they are all properly accounted. For example, the research and development costs of procedures ought to be counted before they are invented, but once they are invented their use, unless there is a patent payment, does not involve cost. When costs are incurred at different times, later costs ought to be discounted. However, these difficulties are not ones of concept so much as problems of ensuring that costs are treated consistently in the calculation of resources expended. The greater conceptual problems come when it is a matter of estimating the benefits of different clinical procedures.

The benefit that clinical procedures produce is better health – or at least that is the intention. Hence in measuring the benefits we are implicitly involved in measuring health improvements. Yet, as we noted earlier, health is a notoriously difficult concept to define. How then can we identify these benefits in any meaningful way? The QALY approach begins with the obvious thought that adding to somebody's years of life is a health benefit. So in measuring the comparative benefits that different procedures produce, we ought to count added years of life within the benefit. There are three respects in which Professor Williams takes this thought further.

In the first place an explicit decision has to be made about the value of added years to different persons. Professor Williams is an egalitarian in this respect. For him an extra year of life is equally valuable irrespective of who is the beneficiary. It does not matter whether you are rich or poor, young or old, high-born or low-born. A year of life is a year of life. It is possible to think of a number of justifications for this approach, but it is perhaps sufficient to say that in a democratic society it would be difficult to propose some other basis of valuation without running into severe embarrassment. Democratic societies must guarantee some minimal formal equality to their members, and it would be difficult to imagine any explicit principle of discrimination between different types of persons gaining public acceptance. For our part, we are happy to endorse Professor Williams's thinking, while reserving judgment as to whether the overall approach does not unwittingly entrench forms of discrimination that violate equality in other, and potentially more serious, ways.

The second reason why it is not sufficient simply to count the number of years of added life stems from attitudes towards the future. It is common in the appraisal of public projects to regard future benefits as of lower value than present benefits. The argument is that the postponement of a benefit has a cost which ought to be subtracted from the value of the benefit in order to produce a valid estimate of how much it is worth giving up now in order to achieve a benefit in the future. The factor by which the future benefit is discounted is known as the discount rate, and it will be necessary in any economic approach to other problems to priorities to ensure that future benefits are appropriately discounted. It will also be necessary to increase the discount factor in the face of uncertainty. If one procedure gives a low probability of a large number of extra years and another procedure gives a high probability of a few number of extra years, it would obviously be a mistake to count the years in the same way. We need instead to take into account the probability that the years promised will actually be enjoyed. This uncertainty in the expectation of benefit also needs to be taken into account.

The third reason why something other than merely added years should be taken into account when assessing the benefits of different clinical procedures arises from considerations of quality of life. The reason for including this requirement is not difficult to find. Suppose there is a procedure that promises to save the same number of lives as some other procedure, but it yields a higher quality of life per patient treated. Then we should clearly have reason to prefer that procedure. The quality of life needs to be reckoned in our estimate of the benefit, and it seems difficult to dispute in principle that added years should be 'quality adjusted' if we are to have an adequate estimate of

57

the effects of different clinical procedures. The problems arise not at the level of principle, but in trying to devise a method by which quality of life can be meaningfully assessed. It is over the resolution of this issue that any proposal to assess the benefits of clinical procedures is likely to be most controversial.

The approach favoured by Professor Williams is to construct an index of quality of life from the subjective evaluations of persons in the community. At present these evaluations are derived solely from psychometric investigations with small selected groups of individuals, and therefore it is difficult to know how such indices might be constructed to be of more general use. However, the results so far provide sufficient material to illustrate the logic of the approach and it is worth considering the results in some detail (Kind, Rosser and Williams, 1982).

Individuals participating in the research are provided with a set of 29 states involving disability and distress which they are required to consider. By means of a system of elaborate interviews they can rank these illness states relative to one another, and can express their rankings in the form of a ratio scale. That is to say, they will not only express preferences over the available states, but they are also able to say by how much one state is worth less or more than another. For example, in one sample the average evaluation made the state 'choice of work or performance at work very severely limited and mild distress' equal to 'severe social disability and/or slight impairment of performance at work and moderate distress', and both of these states were regarded as being some 96 per cent as good as being fit. In general, if fitness is valued at 1 and death at 0, then it is possible to obtain consistent and coherent rankings of alternative health states, including the possibility that some states are ranked worse than death.

Assuming that these relative evaluations mean something, it is possible to use the values that emerge in order to estimate the benefits that flow from various clinical procedures. It may be useful to give an idea of the magnitudes which emerge from a cost-benefit analysis of different procedures, and some illustrative figures for the control of coronary heart disease are given in Table 3 (page 59). It can be seen from the table that different procedures produce different results in terms of cost-per-QALY saved. For the purposes of comparison it is useful to compare the QALY cost for other procedures and other diseases. Professor Williams estimates that kidney transplantation generates a cost-per-QALY of about £3200 and heart transplantation a cost of about £8000. Hospital haemodialysis probably costs between £15,000 and £20,000 per QALY.

Table 3   Costs-per-QALY of procedures relating to coronary heart disease

Procedure	Cost-per-QALY (£'000)
Advice by GPs to stop smoking	0.18
Action by GPs to control hypertension	1.70
GP control of serum cholesterol	1.70
CABG for severe angina with LMD	1.04
CABG for severe angina with 3VD	1.27
CABG for moderate angina with LMD	1.33
CABG for severe angina with 2VD	2.28

CABG = coronary artery bypass graft; 2VD = 2 vessel disease;
3VD = 3 vessel disease; LMD = left main disease.

PROBLEMS WITH THE ECONOMIC APPROACH

There is no doubt that the QALY approach can be illuminating. Organisations are creatures of habit, and often they ignore the task of seeing whether their regular habits are the best way of achieving the purposes they set themselves. New procedures may find it difficult to gain a place in the established routines, and when it is a question of considering policy alternatives across administrative boundaries, for example the boundary that divides hospital-based services from the primary care services, it is necessary to have an approach that is capable of considering issues at a high level of generality. Moreover, provided that the estimation of QALYs does not become a substitute for judgment, we find it difficult to believe that policy makers who are concerned to deliver high quality care in a fair minded way would not want information on the cost of different procedures as an aid to their decision making. The QALY approach aspires to provide such information on the most comprehensive basis, and is therefore to be welcomed for that reason. At an absolute minimum, the wide differences and the rankings raise good questions about relative priorities.

However, there are severe problems with the approach, and it is as well that these are frankly recognised, particularly as they are intrinsic to the approach as advocated. Five problems especially seem worthy of attention: the source of the valuations of different health states; the variability of these valuations across different individuals; the problem of whether there is not an implicit discrimination against certain patient-groups in the approach; the meaning of the information that QALYs yield; and the way in which the approach equates need with the ability to benefit.

The source of the valuations is a problem because there is no reason to expect that different groups will rank health states in the same way, and there is therefore a problem in knowing which valuation to use. Professor Williams and his colleagues report results from six different groups: medical patients; psychiatric patients; medical nurses; psychiatric nurses; healthy volunteers; and doctors (Kind, Rosser and Williams, 1982). There is not a high degree of consensus between the evaluations, particularly when it is a matter of assessing the high disability/high distress states. Any policy maker who wishes to use the approach will therefore need to make an explicit selection of the reference group whose valuations will be used. If the aim of the approach is to reflect community values in the allocation of resources, the policy maker is confronted with the fact that the values chosen will not be those of the community at large, but of a particular subset of the population. Such a situation clearly runs the risk that the policy maker will substitute his or her own values for those of the community by selecting that reference group whose values seem most congenial.

The problem presented by the source of the valuations is compounded by the problem of variability. Even if there were a consensus of values to emerge among different groups in the population, there would still be a variability of individuals around the group average, and possibly a variability of the same individuals as they encounter different life experiences. Professor Williams and his associates report large variability within groups, and the results they have documented represent the median evaluation by members of the specific group. In turn this gives rise to the problem presented by minority tastes. If the community evaluation is based on the average of some representative group's evaluation, then minorities whose tastes deviate sharply from those in the same group will to that extent be disadvantaged. The allocation of resources that stems from the assessment of quality adjusted life years will reflect the number of people who value outcomes in a certain way. It may be argued that it is no worse, and in some ways may be better, for the authoritative evaluation to arise from a community average rather than from a planner's preferences or from the accumulated commitments of the past – but that in itself is a contentious proposition. The problem is also eased by the existence of private health care which those with minority tastes, and with sufficient resources, can use if they so desire. Yet this is no more than a second best solution to a problem that seems intrinsic to the QALY approach.

The third difficulty is more complex, and we cannot do it justice in a short space, but it concerns the possibility of discrimination. As presented, the QALY approach is formally egalitarian: a year is a year no matter who is the beneficiary. However, as the calculations of benefit are constructed, it may turn out that the recommendations have the effect of slanting resources away from certain groups and towards others. This possibility is illustrated in Table 3 (page 59). One of the reasons why the preventive proposals seem a better buy on average is that they cut the incidence of heart disease among the lower age groups, so that the cumulative effect of the additional life years is very considerable. If in consequence resources are switched away from surgical procedures and into preventive measures, then members of the older age groups may feel justified in complaining that their interests have been unfairly underweighted in the balance. It should be clear in the general case that any procedure that involves counting extra years of life as part of the benefit of medical procedures will risk shifting resources away from the elderly and towards younger age groups – contrary, it may be noticed, to the stated policy of successive British governments.

The QALY approach is subject, allegedly, to other forms of discrimination. In respect of life-saving measures the use of QALYs disadvantages those with a low quality of life compared with those with a high quality. This discrimination formally parallels the problem of age discrimination. Just as the bias against the elderly reflects the counting of an added quantity of life-years, so the bias against those with a low quality of life reflects the quality adjustment to that quantity. Both effects, it may be noticed, have the disturbing characteristic that they will lead to switching resources away from those in most immediate medical need – contrary to the injunctions of traditional medical ethics and the instincts of most physicians, other health care professionals and, indeed, people in general. It is worth noting, however, that it is in principle no different from medical triage on the battlefield where the instinct to help those in greatest need is overridden by considerations of maximum benefit. There will always be tension between the desire to make great efforts and use considerable resources to save the life of one seriously ill or endangered patient (even where the probability of success is low) and the desire to distribute the same effort and resources more widely at the expense of the one for the greater benefit of the many. QALYs do not acknowledge this tension.

What are we to make of this apparently extensive discrimination in the allocation of resources enjoined by the QALY approach? The issues need to be treated carefully. Although QALYs disadvantage those with low quality of life in respect of life-saving measures, they confer advantage on the same persons in respect of quality-enhancing treatments (Menzel, 1987, page 3). If there is a bias in the QALY approach, we should not expect that bias to play itself out in obvious, or identifiably vicious, ways across patient-groups. Moreover, it has been argued that the only way in which we can be fair between different individuals is to use the device of a lottery (Harris, 1987); but it is far from obvious to us that the procedural fairness that might be gained by the lottery approach outweighs the gain in outcome benefit that a rational use of QALYs promises.

One way around the charge of discrimination is to say that the correct point of view from which to assess the allocation of resources is not by inspecting the relative needs of different patient-groups at any one point in time, but to examine the health needs of individuals as they would be rationally assessed over the whole of their lifetimes. If those individuals who provide the data used to construct QALYs are actually saying that they attach more importance to quality-enhancement for a given span of years than to extending that span, it seems a mere imposition of planners' preferences to assert different priorities.

It is at this point that the fourth difficulty with QALYs emerges. When individuals express views about alternative health status outcomes, do we have any reason to treat these views as reasons for adopting one public policy rather than another? When individuals volunteer the view that they prefer a shorter, healthier life to a longer, less healthy one, are they thereby committed to a generalisable prescription to the effect that public agencies ought to prefer quality-enhancing measures to quantity-increasing ones? It would seem not, for individuals could always argue that though they preferred quality improvements for themselves, this was no reason for giving their quantity-increasing treatments lower priority than others' quality-enhancing ones. Personal preferences about the form one's own life should take do not yield social judgments about how lives in general are to be treated.

This objection to the use of QALYs is undoubtedly valid, but it is important to understand what it does, and does not, imply. It implies that it would not be proper to move from a statement of how members of a community valued different sorts of lives to a prescription about the priorities that public policy should pursue. It does not imply that QALY information is not a useful, and perhaps essential, consideration for policy makers who have the authority to make public decisions. If those with the authority to make public decisions based their judgment, in part at least, on considerations that stem from QALY statements that by itself that would not, in our opinion, invalidate the policy.

There is a fifth difficulty with QALYs. They equate the concept of need with the ability to benefit – the more one can benefit from X the more one needs X. This fails to offer any weighting to favour those whose needs stem from great misfortune – especially, in our context, medical misfortune – over those whose 'needs' consist simply of a capacity to benefit. Most of us could benefit, perhaps very considerably, from holidays in the resorts of our choice, but most of us also believe that scarce resources should be used for caring for the seriously ill rather than for holidays, even if *far more* QALYs could be gained by forgetting about the sick and providing more holidays.

The reason for our opinion is that decision makers must balance the various competing claims, among the the tension referred to earlier between making enormous efforts at great expense (perhaps with low probability of success) for those in great medical need, and those in less need who can benefit more with less effort and expense and thus in larger numbers. On some occasions a just allocation of resources will require the latter rather than the former, and QALYs, if suitably developed, would enable decision-makers to weigh up the benefits of competing alternative courses of action. They should never *replace* such weighing up, however agonising; for equally, we believe there should always be some room for the special and enormous effort for those in greatest need, even where this does *not* maximise QALY gain.

Care has to be taken in using QALYs. Since they are intellectual constructs that incorporate particular values, it is misleading to suppose that they offer a neutral, merely technical means of making policy. Moreover, their practical significance falls behind the sophistication of the discussion that has occurred over their proper use; there are still considerable methodological problems involved in their development. However, we do not see how any health policy that is sensitive to the issues of resource allocation can dispense with considerations that reflect both the length and the quality of life that people can expect from treatment.

OTHER METHODS FOR ACHIEVING EFFICIENCY

Although the development of QALYs is the most ambitious programme for seeking gains in the efficiency with which resources are used, there are other approaches that should be noted if only to make clear that their more modest scope does not free them entirely from ethical issues. The essence of these alternative approaches is to focus upon the cost side of clinical procedures, leaving out any estimation of the relative benefits these procedures produce. A clear example is provided by the use of 'diagnostic related groups' (DRGs), which became part of the USA's Medicare programme in 1983 and have created some interest more generally.

The approach using DRGs seeks to identify clinical conditions in such a way that meaningful average cost information can be provided for each of these conditions. This information on cost can be used as a yardstick by which to measure variations in the cost of treatment that occur in practice. Clearly no information is thereby obtained on the benefits of the treatment provided, but it is possible to identify whether, for any condition, treatment is being provided as efficiently as the cost norm implies. The information can then be used as part of a prospective payments system with the intention of encouraging providers to reduce the costs of their treatments. Thus, the US Medicare programme no longer reimburses hospitals, as it once did, the costs that they have actually incurred, but pays them instead according to the average cost of comparable hospitals in the nation and region. Within this system, hospitals bear some of the financial risk associated with treating patients, but they realise a surplus if the payments they receive exceed their costs. The risk stick and the financial carrot are intended to provide an incentive for hospitals to improve their efficiency.

Those responsible for the finance of health care need to ensure that they are obtaining good value for money, and part of the attraction of DRGs is that they have seemed to offer an automatic mechanism for achieving this end. By using a prospective payments system built upon DRGs, it seems as though there is a clear incentive for providers to economise on the resources they use. Those who purchase care, therefore, have an independent check upon providers' costs and a device by which to induce a more economical use of resources. Despite these advantages, however, there are problems with the use of DRGs which have been revealed on the basis of early experience (see Inglehart, 1986; Office of Technology Assessment, 1983).

The central problem of DRGs is that, although they provide hospitals with an incentive to economise on resources, they thereby provide an incentive for hospitals to manipulate the payments scheme by substituting more expensive diagnoses for less expensive and by undertaking some activities rather than others. When operating effectively, DRGs should be constructed to ensure that prices are set in a way that reflects the relative value of each diagnostic group, otherwise hospitals will have an incentive to manipulate the case mix and concentrate on the more remunerative items. One barrier preventing this equalisation across DRGs is the difficulty of identifying, let alone measuring, efficient and clinically optimal patient care. Moreover, since technological innovation is rapid in some areas of practice, there is a need for a continual adjustment in the estimation of DRGs. There is also a need to ensure that the use of DRGs does not inhibit the appropriate introduction of new, but cost-raising, technologies. This is a particularly acute problem because the absence of benefit information means that added costs cannot be compared to added benefits. Finally, and most seriously, is the danger that the use of DRGs will lower the quality of care. Evidence from the US on this point is fragmentary and impressionistic, but it does suggest that there is pressure under the incentive of DRGs, for example, to discharge early (Inglehart, 1986, page 1464). A balance has to be struck between the responsible stewardship of resources and the quality of care given to individual patients, and there is clearly a danger that the use of DRGs will bias decisions systematically in the direction of too much economy at the expense of quality of care.

None of this is to say that DRG studies should be ended, or that it is wrong to experiment with such techniques in appropriate ways to see whether they can be refined in order to improve cost control. It does suggest caution, however, and an honest intention to fund the study of the effects of particular versions of the DRG approach to assess their effects. Moreover, the evidence that we have suggests that programmes of quality assurance are needed to counteract the incentives of the per-case payment system to skimp the quality of services (Office of Technology Assessment, 1983, page 7). In our view, it would be irresponsible to implement a policy of DRG control, or its equivalent, without a simultaneous commitment of resources to ensure that the quality of care was not jeopardised.

The problems of implementing DRGs do not mean, however, that no advance can be made in improving efficiency. One obvious route forward is to pursue more cost-effectiveness studies. Such studies seek to identify which, from a range of treatments, is most cost-effective in treating a particular condition. Such studies have revealed wide variations in the cost of treating specified conditions without there being an apparent variation of clinical benefit (cited in Abel-Smith, 1976, page 116). In the mechanisms for allocating financial resources there need to be incentives to maximise effectiveness. Moreover, it is possible to disseminate information on cost-effectiveness by means of peer-review of the sort we identified in the previous chapter. In the absence of any mechanical scheme of financial incentives that will improve efficiency, the responsible use of cost-effectiveness information in the process of peer-review promises improvements in efficiency not obtainable by other means.

The Search for Accountability

The argument we have pursued is that the ethical dilemmas of resource allocation demand a public appeal to the values contained within our civic culture. According to this account, the process by which ethical disagreements are arbitrated is important in showing the good faith of the public authorities in respect of the trust from society which they hold. Governments need to convince as well as decide.

In undertaking this task they are mediating between the three groups who ultimately have to share the burdens of cost-control, namely patients, providers and citizens as financers. As we have already noted, none of these groups has automatic priority and governments must seek to convince them that their legitimate demands and aspirations are being weighed and considered. Respect for the often hard decisions that have to be taken will be enhanced if it is clear that such decisions reflect considerations of the interests of members of these groups rather than being merely devices for avoiding political embarrassment or the pursuit of partisan ideology. To convince in policy making is harder, but ultimately more worthwhile, than to decide by reference to prior conviction.

Perhaps the greatest test of this approach arises from the fundamental issues of structure and finance. The main burden of health care in the UK is carried by the NHS, a tax-funded public institution in which the ownership and control of resources is vested with a variety of public authorities. Some critics have seen its structure as the source of its weakness. It is argued that such an institutional form is unsuitable for health care. Those who are happy with public ownership and control are often unhappy with the volume of resources that are devoted to the NHS. There are others who are unhappy with the distribution of resources between different geographical areas. So it is to these fundamental issues – structure, finance and the distribution of resources – that we turn in this chapter.

STRUCTURE

If it is accepted that health and health care have a special value and enjoy a privileged status, the provision of health care to the whole

66

population must be regarded as a public responsibility. All developed societies accept such a responsibility, but the problem is to decide how it should be discharged, and how to resolve the disagreements about which principles of justice to accept and the consequent type of health care system to adopt.

It is helpful when making judgments on these matters to note that health care ranges from life-saving measures to minor life-quality enhancing procedures (Maxwell, 1987). Most people would attach quite different social priority to the meeting of needs that vary across such a wide range. The rationing of dialysis facilities for end-stage renal failure justifiably causes more anxiety and disquiet than the rationing of surgical facilities for the removal of tattoos. Somewhere in the spectrum from the critical to the minor a decision has to be taken about the extent of public responsibility and the degree of seriousness that it involves. There is no purely logical way of deciding where on this spectrum public responsibility is crucial. This does not mean that the allocation of public responsibility is arbitrary merely because its extent cannot be defined with precision (any more than the difficulty of defining hair-loss means that we cannot distinguish the bald from the hirsute), but it does mean that we should be careful in our judgments of structure to relate the responsibilities of provision to the seriousness of the health demand that is involved.

A further general point to note is the clear distinction that exists between the financing of a service and the provision of a service. Public responsibility for health care need not imply public owner-ship of health care facilities. A useful illustration of this is the distinction between Sweden and the Netherlands. Both spend a relatively high proportion of their GDP on health care: Sweden spends 9.3 per cent and the Netherlands spends 8.3 per cent. Both countries are generally reckoned to perform well on measures of health status. Yet in Sweden health facilities, including those concerned with primary care, are owned by the government, whereas in the Netherlands there is wide variety in the ownership of such facilities, with ownership vested in legally independent private associations controlling some 90 per cent of hospitals in 1980 (Rutten and van der Werff, 1982, page 178).

A final important distinction is between inequalities of health care arising from the workings of a structure and inequalities of health care built into the design of such a structure. It is well known that a great many health care inequalities persist in the NHS despite its 40 years of operation. These inequalities may arise from the workings of the service in ways that are still poorly understood. However, the

NHS aspires to treat its patients even-handedly, and is therefore in quite a different category from, say, the US Medicare programme that is designed on the premise that there should be distinct levels and types of service for the poor. In the NHS the inequalities that exist are not a consequence of public choices made within the political system in a way that holds for the two-tier US system of care.

It has been argued (Engelhardt, 1986, page 337) that there are strong reasons for seeking to design a structure of health care so that it meets four objectives: the provision of comprehensive care; the provision of equal care for those with equal needs; protection of choice on the part of health care providers and consumers; and control of health care costs. These objectives do not stand in any straightforward relationship to the principles we have advanced, but they are clearly consistent with those principles and in some respects flow from them. Thus a concern for autonomy requires a concern both for freedom of choice (obviously) and for cost control (less obviously, but related to the ability of persons to control all aspects of their lives and not simply to be hostages to health expenditures). Similarly, a concern for justice implies equal care for equal needs, and the goal of comprehensive care may be related to the principle of beneficence. So it will be useful when considering issues of structure to examine the Engelhardt criteria in some detail.

It is worth bearing in mind that no health care system so far designed scores top marks in all four dimensions of consideration. Those that are good on cost containment, such as Canada and the UK, tend to score poorly on freedom of choice; those that are good on the level of care, for example Sweden or Germany, tend to score poorly on cost containment; and there is no convincing evidence that any system scores highly in terms of equality. Some systems, for example that of the US, tend to do badly in a number of dimensions. Moreover, it is perhaps easier to avoid the mistakes of other systems than to copy their successes. Consequently, we should recognise that, when we apply ethical considerations to the appraisal of the structure of health care systems, we are always likely to have to compromise on the absolute demands that any particular value might make upon us.

The form that this compromise might take can be illustrated by reference to Figure 1 (page 69). In this figure we have laid out Engelhardt's four desirata of a health care system in terms of four poles. Any particular system can be mapped onto these four poles depending upon how well it scores in the four dimensions. For the sake of illustration, we have mapped our perception of the UK's and

Figure 1   The trade-offs of health care financing

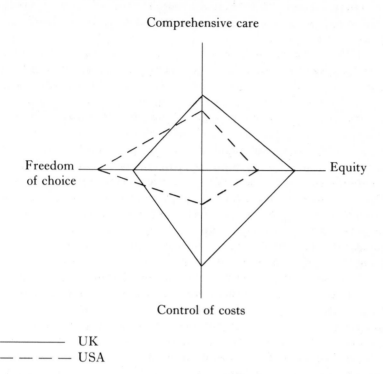

Comprehensive care

Freedom of choice

Equity

Control of costs

——————— UK
— — — — USA

USA's health care systems so that they can be compared. Traditionally, the UK has done well on equity and cost control, but not so well on freedom of choice and comprehensiveness of care; by contrast the USA has done well on freedom of choice and comprehensiveness of care, but not so well on equity and economy. The task of health policy is to improve performance of the system in all four of these dimensions, but at any one time it may be impossible to achieve improvements in any one respect without sacrificing advantages in another.

In practice, the conflicts that arise can be seen in the trade-offs that confront attempts to improve the NHS. Increasing freedom of choice may threaten not only the equity objective but also the objective of controlling costs. Providing comprehensive care is clearly often at odds with controlling costs, and may reduce equity as novel and expensive treatments become available in only a limited number of outlets. It may even be that there can be a decline in one dimension without a corresponding improvement in another dimension. As a group, for example, our perception is that comprehensiveness of care in the UK has declined in recent years with only small improvements in other dimensions of concern, for example geographical inequalities.

What does this mean in practice? A recent review of health finance options has urged that there is no perfect system that can meet all the demands that are placed upon it, and that the challenge confronting policy-makers is to seek ways of reducing imperfections, taking the existing NHS as the starting-point (Robinson, 1988, page 25). We should like to endorse that conclusion noting that a concern for ethical values should not preclude the exploration of far-reaching options for change. For example, there is no reason of principle why there should not be a greater separation between the finance of care and provision for care, which in practice might involve turning health authorities more into purchasers of health services rather than providers. Ethical principles do not imply endorsement of any particular institutional arrangement. However, it would be unethical to experiment with new institutional forms without taking care to monitor what changes result and without noting the evidence relevant to their evaluation that already exists. For example, we have already (pages 63–65) drawn attention to the problems involved in using DRGs, and any attempt further to separate finance and provision in the NHS is obliged to show how it will avoid these problems. Similarly, the exploration of far-reaching options should not jeopardise the achievements of the NHS, most notably its relative success in creating an equality of status for those who are its patients.

RESOURCES

The hardest questions (the most intractable and emotive) in the ethics of resource allocation in health care arise at the margins of the system's resources. Questions then arise as to which patients shall receive care and which shall not. However, there are a series of problems that arise in the determination of the constraints that operate at the margin. In particular, there is the issue of underfunding or overfunding. How might we discover whether decisions at the margin are too tightly constrained or not subject to sufficient discipline? In particular, how might we discover whether the NHS was properly resourced?

This question may be partly answered in terms of four main indicators. Firstly, international comparisons between the UK and other societies at a comparable level of economic development can help demonstrate what proportions of GDP a developed economy can sustain on health care expenditure, and what mix of resources and services can be provided for that expenditure. Secondly, waiting times for access to health care, and the numbers of people waiting, are *prima facie* evidence of under-resourcing, assuming that existing resources are being used more or less efficiently. These indications are especially telling in regard to conditions for which effective treatments are already widely technically available, and if they persist and grow over long periods. Thirdly, rising demand for private health care in basic and routine matters such as hip replacements is a function of an under-resourced public health service. The trend is especially serious when this demand shifts towards life-saving or disability-preventing treatments. Clearly, this indicator understates the resource constraints in public health services because (notoriously) not all the needs for care can be expressed as in the form of market demand. Fourthly, salary levels for public health staff can be compared with their counterparts in the private sector and abroad. Relatively low salary levels in the public sector suggest that some costs of under-resourcing public health care are borne by staff not users.

The allocation of funds should be such that appropriate and proven life-saving treatment is not withheld, and that appropriate and proven measures which reduce morbidity are available within a reasonable period of time from the onset of symptoms. The increasing proportion of treatment for the latter reason being provided by the private sector has an obvious effect on the sums required from government sources. The short-fall of funds for what could be achieved forces decision-makers to face ethical choices at every level: at the national level where the total sum is decided, and where extra sums can be made available to meet new contingencies (for example, HIV infection); at the subsequent institutional level where the size of a region's or district's facilities are decided (for example, the number of psychogeriatric beds or the extent of the screening for cervical cancer); and finally at the point at which an individual's treatment is decided, either by active intervention or by a decision to refer for specialist advice and possible treatment.

There will, of course, always be controversy about the total volume of resources that ought to be devoted to health care, in all its forms, from national income. It is sometimes tempting to seek to detach decisions about the level of funding from such controversy – for example, by relating health expenditure to some fixed proportion of national income (O'Higgins, 1987). However, we believe there is an alternative point of view based on the principle of accountability

71

that we have sought to develop. In particular, it is the task of those responsible for financing the system to explain their expectations about the volume and quality of care that can be produced at the chosen level of resources. Equally, it is the task of those who manage or work in the system to explain why some expectations might be unreasonable and what contribution they see themselves making to the attainment of generally agreed objectives. Finally, it is the task of the public to participate in the debate about the appropriate levels of service that may be provided and to exercise their political rights in determining which party is best placed to discharge its self-appointed obligations. It is worth illustrating what each of these tasks might mean in practice.

At any one time the government of the day makes a series of decisions about the volume of resources that should be devoted to health care. What the existing mechanisms of political accountability fail to do is to place a constraint upon government to explain its expectations about the health care that will be delivered with its chosen volume of resources. Consequently the rationing decisions that are implicit in the choices that governments make about resources are rarely if ever made explicit, either to the health service or to the public at large. This is most painfully true in relation to dialysis for end-stage renal failure, where the age-rationing that is practised is seldom discussed in public. But it is also true in relation to quality of life issues, for example hip replacements, where underfunding leads to over-economising on a proven and beneficial procedure.

It is, of course, the responsibility of health authorities to spend the resources that they are' allocated, but this should not prevent the government from explaining systematically and clearly what it expects about the volume and quality of care that a well-functioning authority should provide. This would enable health authorities and the public to be aware of the obligations and the opportunities that are implied by national funding decisions, and it would provide a yardstick against which to measure the adequacy or otherwise of the funding provided. At present it is too easy for government to pass down the line the human and resource consequences of decisions that have been taken without regard to their feasibility and practicality.

An approach along these lines would resemble the recommendations made by Sir Roy Griffiths in his review of community care policy (Griffiths, 1988). His proposals were that a minister of state in the DHSS should have the role of preparing and publishing a statement of objectives and priorities, laying down and reviewing service standards, making arrangements for the reviewing of activity and *ensuring the necessary matching between policy objectives and the resources provided to meet them*. Our stress on this last aspect of the Griffiths proposals reflects our view that the central way in which accountability is responsibly discharged is to ensure that there is a public process by which resources are matched to agreed standards. Unless that matching is done in an open and explicit way there is always the danger that services will be under-resourced, and that dishonesty about funding will prevail.

It may be argued that it is unrealistic to expect governments to become accountable in this way, since it is an immensely difficult and complex task to say what is implicit in a particular allocation. However, there are models on which to draw for experience. Thus, in the system of German social insurance, it is necessary for the insurers to state explicitly what is and is not covered, just as private insurers in the UK must state in their policies what treatments or conditions were excluded by the terms of the contract. If UK governments were made accountable for stating the package of health benefits that the typical citizen might expect at any given level of public expenditure (in other words, to define a citizen's health care package) they would have less room for manoeuvre in fudging the, admittedly difficult, issues. There is nothing unjust or indefensible in a government saying that there are certain treatments that cannot be afforded or, because of their expense and novelty, will only be available in parts of the health service (as, for example, with *in vitro* fertilisation). There is dishonesty in pretending to finance comprehensive health care when even efficient health authorities find they have cumulative problems in meeting reasonable expectations of care.

One advantage of making governments more accountable in this manner is that it provides a context within which the pursuit of greater efficiency and effectiveness becomes possible. Changing the character of clinical freedom to create a willingness to examine the effectiveness of treatments will be helped if the government is seen to be acting responsibly by giving an account of its expectations in relation to a given body of funding. The search for effectiveness could then be seen for what it should be, namely an attempt by government and the NHS to ensure that treatments are worth their cost, rather than a device for escaping from the unpleasant political consequences of underfunding. Since it will be necessary to define what treatments and procedures are effective, before making a rational decision about what to include in the package, securing consent to examining effectiveness becomes the means by which improvements can be sought.

73

A similar point can be made about efficiency. Health authorities have found in recent years that more efficient ways of treating patients can lead to financial penalties, since the decrease in unit cost secured is outweighed by the increase in total costs that a greater throughput implies. Moreover, cost improvement programmes have been criticised in some cases for worsening the level of service under the guise of achieving improvements in efficiency, and this is clearly a constant danger as long as the content of the package that citizens can expect is never specified. One advantage of the concept, therefore, is that it disentangles the search for efficiency from the content of care that is delivered to patients.

A final advantage of the proposal is that it would provide a vehicle for educating the public about the costs and benefits of various alternative packages of finance and provision. If it is true that more could be spent to good effect on health than we currently spend, it is equally true that there must come a point where no prudent person would think it of value to spend more. At present, information is presented to the public in such a way as to disguise this fact. An explicit attempt to relate benefits to costs would do much to raise the tone of public debate.

We do not pretend that reform of our current practice is without difficulties. Clearly we would expect a great deal of controversial debate about what should and should not be included in the citizens' health care package. Drawing boundaries is rarely an easy task. If we say hip replacements are included, do we also say that knee replacements are included? Evidence shows a low use by UK clinicians of chemotherapy for metastatic cancers: should there be an explicit decision not to include such treatments? How would rationing for end-stage renal failure be justified in public terms? How could one avoid the resistance to new treatments being included because they were expensive initially even though in the long term they seemed promising? Where is the line to be drawn between minor cosmetic surgery and surgery that significantly enhances the quality of someone's life? These and other questions would have to be tackled in defining the citizens' health care package. Moreover, there would have to be a national programme for developing and evaluating new treatments to ensure that they provide good value for money.

In this context it may be worth noting that present policies involve the drawing of lines. Thus health authorities have to decide what is acceptable and what is not acceptable by way of income generation. As well as the conventional measures of income generation that involve retailing goods and services in hospitals, it would also be possible to generate income by offering medical services in certain areas, for example sports' injuries. These are the types of condition whose terms of eligibility would have to be debated; but in principle that debate is no different from the one that currently takes place within the system. A similar point can be made by noting that certain treatments or conditions may be included in the package under some terms but not others. Thus expensive therapies might be included if they were part of a research protocol, but not if they were simply being pursued without a serious attempt to assess their effectiveness.

Our present system does not avoid such questions, but treats them instead in an implicit, inarticulated and haphazard form. To make such choices openly is the prerequisite to discharging the obligation to act in a morally defensible manner.

DISTRIBUTION

The previous two sections have argued that public responsibility for health care is unavoidable and that it should aim to meet the reasonable expectations of citizens. This approach bases claims to access to health on citizenship combined with the judgment of a certified medical practitioner about one's state of need. However, there are ethical questions to be raised not only about the total volume of resources that might be justifiably devoted to health care but also about the distribution of those resources among those who might benefit from those resources. In recent years many hospital districts have seen their resources decline as much from redistribution as from absolute shortage of funds. Thus, two of the examples we cited in chapter 1 fell into this category. The issues surrounding the ethics of redistribution are as sharp and difficult in practical terms as they are theoretically.

Because access to health care is based upon claims of citizenship, there is a widespread feeling that this implies equality of provision for people with equal needs. If justice entails treating equals equally, then the fact of common citizenship provides the grounds for ensuring that all citizens have access to facilities of a similar type and standard. Moreover, this view is widely shared within developed societies, to the point of incorporating into policy targets the principle that the provision of facilities should aim to equalise health status among members of the population. For example, Health for All by the Year 2000 has as its first target a 25 per cent reduction in the differences in health status between groups within countries as well as between countries (Faculty of Community Medicine, 1986). Justice in this context means that persons should be given their due

75

in terms of services relevant to certified medical need, and that the basis for similar treatment should be common citizenship. Justice is equality in relation to a norm of what citizens can expect as of right from their governments.

In practice policy-makers use a variety of ad hoc proxy measures as a way of assessing how well health services are meeting the test of equality. Priority may be given to particular patient groups – for example, the mentally ill or handicapped – in an attempt to target a population subgroup that is thought to be especially vulnerable. RAWP is used to redistribute the resources that underlie the inequalities of access imposing differential burdens on some patients. The Black report (see Townsend and Davidson, 1982) draws attention to some particular health status inequalities in identifying variations in age-specific mortality among working-age males. And governments have pursued various policies to reduce waiting lists. From our point of view, what matters is not the precise way in which inequality is measured, for that is the subject of evolving specialist expertise, but instead the direction of movement in policy.

To avoid misunderstanding it may be worth noting what the principle of equality does *not* imply when applied to health care. It does not imply the abolition of specialist national centres of excellence, nor does it preclude making extra resources available for the purposes of teaching and medical education. Such special provision is best conceived as a form of investment, intended to raise standards and levels of performance which will benefit the system as a whole in the long run. It should not be taken entirely on trust, but neither should its potential value be dismissed lightly. It may also be necessary to ensure accountability in the discharge of these various functions, but that is quite a different matter from ignoring the fact that such extra functions require their own resources.

There is a paradox about the pursuit of greater equality. Although it is a principle widely accepted within the health service and health policy, its implementation encounters severe political opposition. It is possible to regard this opposition as merely a symptom of bad faith, looking upon the public acceptance of equality as a form of hypocrisy – the homage that vice pays to virtue. This attitude, however, is one-sided and mistaken. There may be simply the power of vested and entrenched interests opposing redistribution. On the other hand, it is more constructive to see the opposition as motivated by a genuine concern for specific problems encountered in the pursuit of equality and for the values that a naive egalitarianism risks ignoring. In this context it is useful to look at the example of the

RAWP formula, for this formula implies only a modest egalitarianism, requiring the removal of historically determined and apparently arbitrary inequalities of finance.

What, then, are those concerns and values? One cluster of objections arises from the thought that greater equality, at least in any form in which it could practically be implemented, will produce inefficiencies of various sorts. The reduction of resources in London teaching hospitals, for example, may lead to the loss of accumulated expertise and experience that it would take a generation to replace in the regions to which the resources are shifted. Moreover, since it is human skills and energies that are the most important in the delivery of human services, there is likely to be a built-in inefficiency in the shift of resources. For example, the physical plant will be used at first to less good effect by those who lack the habits and familiarity of those working in established areas of excellence. More resources would be needed under these circumstances to deliver a given quantity and quality of service.

The second cluster of objections revolves around the idea of fairness. It has frequently been argued that it is unfair to deprive someone of an existing benefit simply in order to make up a loss to another who has no experience of the benefit. The pain of loss is greater than the pleasure of gain. There is of course no way of knowing whether this principle holds in particular cases. However, the volume and intensity of protest over the closing of London hospitals at least suggests that something of the sort may be operative. Moreover, there is the existence of the private sector. Some of those who are dissatisfied with public provision can buy their way into the private sector, where the effects of the policy of equality are mitigated. Since the private sector is unlikely to disappear, it may be argued that the policy of equality works to the arbitrary advantage of those with money instead of the arbitrary advantage of those who live in a particular part of the country. What, also, of the people who have chosen to live in a particular area because of the quality of its public services? Does not a public policy of redistribution from a fixed base risk being unfair to these people?

It is difficult to know how far one's thinking on these matters ought to be influenced by decisions on the general level of resources going into the health care system. Clearly it is much easier to achieve a narrowing of inequalities in circumstances of general growth: relative gains do not have to be made at the expense of absolute losses. If general resources within the system grow at a rate commensurate to national income, it ought to be possible to improve services in currently deprived sectors. However, if this degree of general growth is not being achieved, then the dilemmas to which the pursuit of inequality gives rise are correspondingly sharpened.

One thing is clear: merely because there are objections of principle to a policy, we cannot conclude that the policy should not be pursued. Values and principles clash in the world of practice, and if a principle is worth upholding it will be worth upholding, in some circumstances at least, against the counter-claims of other principles. Moreover, the value of equality is founded upon the observation that persons are deserving of respect in their own right, as rational agents capable of choice and purpose. The concept of citizenship is meaningless unless it gives the principle of respect for persons a firm and clear role in public institutions.

We are therefore left with the conclusion that equality must receive significant weight in the making of public policy on health matters. We cannot determine in any general way what degree of weight it should be given, but as an indication of our thinking it may be worth saying that we see the value of a RAWP system outweighing its disadvantages even in present straitened circumstances. Unless a concern for equality is given at least that much weight, then its application to health policy threatens to become merely symbolic.

CONCLUSION

There is no simple organisational fix that will resolve the dilemmas of health care structure and finance. Analysts of health policy are too often tempted to work in the 'if only . . ' mould, arguing that 'if only we had an internal market in the NHS' or 'if only we had HMOs' or 'if only the NHS had more money' then everything would be all right. Our approach, by contrast, has been to stress that at the heart of the organisation and administration of health care are the notions of personal and public responsibility. The nature and limits of that responsibility need to be defined and determined in open debate. This does not give a licence to ignore questions of organisational innovation, but it does indicate a necessary condition for defensible decision making. Organisations and the people who build and work them will always be fallible. But in their fallibility they should always seek to be responsible.

CHAPTER 9

Recommendations and Checklists

As a way of making explicit our own expectations, we thought it desirable to summarise our perspective in relation to the three levels of decision-making we have identified. After each summary set of points we list a set of questions we think decision-makers at each level should be asking. Not all the questions will be relevant to every decision-maker, but they provide a checklist that people in responsible positions may find constructively challenging. Put another way, something would be wrong if nobody felt it to be their business to answer uncomfortable questions.

NATIONAL LEVEL

1   Public funding, whether through taxation or insurance, is bound to be a major source of finance for health care in order to ensure access and equity. Government should accept that it is publicly accountable not merely for the amount spent from public funds but for what those funds secure in health care.

2   The health services should meet reasonable need, and government should state explicitly what sort of needs can be met from the volume of resources it determines should be spent on health care.

3   Political accountability should be discharged in a principled way – for example, in terms of the principles of beneficence, non-maleficence, autonomy and justice.

4   Governments must persuade as well as decide, educate as well as allocate, in seeking to promote and protect the nation's health.

The following checklist of questions arises from these principles:

1   What principled basis is used for determining total spending on health care within the public budget? What would be the effect of (say) a 10 per cent increase or reduction in public funding?

2   Which groups have been involved in reaching decisions on spending? Which groups ought to be involved? How do you know that the amount spent is what the public wants? Have you calculated the opportunity cost to the health services of giving priority to other, non-health items, in the public budget?

3   Is there a responsible agent of national policy with a clear view of desirable and attainable standards of service in the main areas of spending? How is that view communicated to patients, providers and the public?

4   When deciding on the scale and pace of change in levels of funding and levels of health care provision, have you assessed effects in terms of autonomy, non-maleficence, beneficence and justice?

5   Do you have a means for ensuring that new procedures represent good value for money? How do you eliminate established procedures whose value is low?

6   Under existing arrangements, what are the least satisfactory aspects of health and health care? Who is losing out? What lines of action might offer the greatest gains in relation to these problems?

7   Do you have a mechanism for improving your decision-making if any of the above answers is inadequate?

INSTITUTIONAL LEVEL

1   Accountability is best discharged by means of due process, in which deficiencies and disagreements are acknowledged, and people accept that the way in which decisions are reached is competent and fair.

2   There should be a persistent attempt to improve procedures and structures of decision-making, and explicit criteria for judging improvements should be formulated.

3   Organisational morale should be sustained, and good performance should not be penalised.

4   Health care should be seen as a response to need, and there should be a progressive attempt to eradicate shortcomings.

The following checklist of questions arises from these principles:

1   Which groups will gain or lose by the decisions you are making on allocation? Are these gains and losses consistent with the principles of autonomy, non-maleficence, beneficence and justice?

2   How do you make your criteria of choice publicly understood?

3   How do you ensure that changes in service levels are economically effective and equitable?

4   How does your performance compare with other similar institutions? Do the differences provide pointers to improvement?

5   How do you safeguard clinicians' autonomy (responsibly exercised) and users' choice?

6   What evidence do you have that the services provided are effective? What are the principal unmet needs, for which groups of people, and what could be done about them?

7   What can be done to improve your decision-making and your public accountability? Do you have a formal means for assessing these from an ethical stand point, for example, an ethics committee?

INDIVIDUAL LEVEL

1   All involved in health care must recognise that resources are limited, so that there must be an ever-present concern for effectiveness and efficiency.

2   Providers should be open to peer challenge and audit if they are to discharge their duty of accountability.

3   Providers must respond to the patients' and consumers' reasonable demands for improvements in the quality of care.

4   Patients and citizens should recognise that they carry responsibility for their own well-being in partnership with providers.

The following checklist of questions for clinicians arises from these principles:

1   How far do you press the sectional interests of your specialism against the overall interest of health care?

2   Do you know what are the total costs of your practice, and what each major type of therapy costs?

3   What is your evidence for assuming that your therapies are effective, and how regularly do you review this evidence?

4   How do you decide whom not to treat?

5   Do you treat like cases as like without resort to irrelevant criteria such as occupation, race and gender?

6   When you are dealing with one patient, do you take the needs of others into account and in what ways?

7   Could you explain matters more clearly to your patients and their families? Do you always work to increase their understanding and their ability to make their own informed choices?

8   Do you play an active part in peer audit and review? What else are you doing to improve your clinical practice?

The following checklist of questions for citizens arises from these principles:

1   If you are a member of a community health council, do you consider the problems of matching resources to improvements in service?

2   If you are a member of a group concerned with specific patient needs, do you press the interests of your group to the detriment of others?

3   As a citizen, do you keep yourself informed about health care issues, and is your concern properly reflected in your political choices and activities?

4   Do you accept responsibility for your own health, so that you do not increase the risk of unnecessarily demanding resources that could be used for others?

CONCLUSION

The above questions are not intended to be a substitute for independent thought but a stimulus to it. Our theme has been that moral responsibility is not the mechanical application of rules, but a conscious process of reflection and questioning within a framework of public accountability. No progress will be made and no lasting improvements in the quality of care sustained unless there is a responsible discharge of the duty to allocate health care resources in ways that can stand the test of critical scrutiny.

References

Aaron, Henry and Schwartz, William B (1984) The painful prescription: rationing hospital care. Washington DC, The Brookings Institution.

Abel-Smith, Brian (1976) Value for money in health services. London, Heinemann.

Chalmers, Ian (1986) Minimizing harm and maximizing benefit during innovation in health care: controlled or uncontrolled experimentation? Birth, 13, 3: pp 155–64.

Childress, James F and Beauchamp, Tom L (1983) Principles of biomedical ethics. Oxford, Oxford University Press.

Cochrane, A L (1972) Effectiveness and efficiency: random reflections on health services. London, Nuffield Provincial Hospitals Trust.

Crossman, Richard (1977) The diaries of a cabinet minister, volume 3. London, Hamish Hamilton and Jonathan Cape.

Daniels, Norman (1985) Just health care. Cambridge, Cambridge University Press.

Day, Patricia and Klein, Rudolf (1987) Accountabilities. London, Tavistock.

Engelhardt Jnr, H (1986) The foundations of bioethics. Oxford, Oxford University Press.

Evans, Robert G (1982) Health care in Canada: patterns of funding and regulation. In: McLachlan, G and Maynard, A (eds) The public/private mix for health. London, Nuffield Provincial Hospitals Trust: pp 369–424.

Evans, Robert G (1986) The spurious dilemma: reconciling medical progress and cost control. Quarterly Journal of Health Service Management, 4, 1: pp 25–34.

Faculty of Community Medicine (1986) Health for all by the year 2000: charter for action. London, Faculty of Community Medicine.

83

Fry, Geoffrey K (1986) Inside Whitehall. In: Drucker, Henry and others. Developments in British politics 2. London, Macmillan: pp 88–106.

Griffiths, Sir Roy (1988) Community care: agenda for action. London, HMSO.

Harris, John (1988) EQALYty. In: Byrne, Peter (ed) Health, rights and resources, King's College studies 1987–8. London, King Edward's Hospital Fund for London: pp 100–27.

Health Care UK (1986) Are the government really spending more on the NHS? Health Care UK 1986. Hermitage, Berkshire, Policy Journals.

The Health Service Journal (1987) The public voices its opinions on the NHS. The Health Service Journal, 2 April: pp 382–83.

Hennessy, Peter (1986) Cabinet. Oxford, Basil Blackwell.

Inglehart, J K (1986) Early experience with prospective payment for hospitals. New England Journal of Medicine, 314, 22: pp 1460–64.

Jowell, R, Witherspoon, S and Brook L (1987) British social attitudes: the 1987 report. Aldershot, Gower.

Kind, Paul, Rosser, Rachel and Williams, Alan (1982) Valuation of quality of life: some psychometric evidence. In: Jones-Lee, M W (ed) The value of life and safety. Oxford, North-Holland: pp 159–70.

The Lancet (1987) Accounting for perioperative deaths. The Lancet, 12 December, no 8572: pp 1369–71.

Lunn, John N and Devlin, M Brendon (1987) Lessons from the confidential enquiry into perioperative deaths in three NHS regions. The Lancet, 12 December, no 8572: pp 1384–86.

Maxwell, Robert J (1981) Health and wealth. Lexington, Mass, D C Heath and Co.

Maxwell, Robert (1987) Private medicine and public policy. In: Harrison, A and Gretton, J (eds) Health care UK 1987. Hermitage, Berkshire, Policy Journals.

Menzel, Paul (1987) Creepy QALYs (unpublished).

Nairne, Sir Patrick (1984) Parliamentary control and accountability. In: Maxwell, Robert and Weaver, Nigel (eds) Public participation in health. London, King Edward's Hospital Fund for London: pp 33–50.

National Audit Office (1986) Value for money developments in the National Health Service. London, House of Commons: p 212.

New England Journal of Medicine (1987) Editorial. New England Journal of Medicine, 36: pp 809–10.

Nightingale, Florence (1863) Notes on hospitals. London, Longman, Green, Longman, Roberts and Green.

Office of Technology Assessment (1983) Diagnostic related groups and the Medicare programme. Washington DC, US Congress.

O'Higgins, Michael (1987) Health spending: a way to sustainable growth. London, Institute of Health Services Management.

Rawls, John (1971) A theory of justice. Oxford, Clarendon.

Robinson, Ray (1988) Health finance: assessing the options. Briefing paper no 4. London, King's Fund Institute.

Robinson, Ray and Judge, Ken (1987) Public expenditure and the NHS: trends and prospects. Briefing paper no 2. London, King's Fund Institute.

Rutten, Frans and van der Werff, Albert (1982) Health policy in the Netherlands: at the crossroads. In: McLachlan, G and Maynard, A (eds) The public/private mix for health. London, Nuffield Provincial Hospitals Trust: pp 167–206.

Schieber, G J and Poullier, J-P (1987) Recent trends in international health care spending. Health Affairs, Fall: pp 105–112.

Townsend, P and Davidson, N (1982) Inequalities in health. Harmondsworth, Penguin.

Williams, Alan (1985) Economics of coronary artery bypass grafting. British Medical Journal, 291: pp 326–29.

Williams, A (1986) Screening for risk of CHD: is it a wise use of resources? In: Oliver, M, Ashley-Miller, M and Wood, D. Screening for risk of coronary heart disease. Chichester, John Wiley and Sons: pp 97–106.

Williams, Alan (undated) Health service efficiency and clinical freedom. London, Nuffield, York Portfolios 2.